The Feminine Intention

Powerful, Profitable and Fabulous!

By Dawn Todd

Copyright © 2014 by Dawn Todd.

All rights reserved. No part of this book or its cover may be reprinted, reproduced, or used in any form or manner without the express permission of the publisher, excepting only brief quotations and images of the cover in reviews, or other noncommercial material that references the book or the author.

First published in the United States of America, 2014.

ISBN: 9780989933520

www.dawntodd.com

Dedication

This book is dedicated to fabulous, wildly successful women everywhere—stay wild!

Thank you to Source-God-Jesus, Bob, Orenda, Jordan, Ashley, Kelly, McKayla, Krista, McKenzie, Cassidy, Chelsea, Brooklyn, Reagan, Holly, Connor, Hailey and of course Cooper.

Special thanks to Leslie … and to life for a great ride.

TABLE OF CONTENTS

Preface III

Introduction V

PART ONE: The Seven Lies We Believed

Chapter 1: Be Perfect 2

Chapter 2: Be Strong 6

Chapter 3: Hurry Up 10

Chapter 4: Try Harder 14

Chapter 5: Please Others 18

Chapter 6: I'm Not Good Enough 22

Chapter 7: Something's Wrong with Me 25

Chapter 8: The Origins of the Seven Lies 29

PART TWO: The Kuan Yin Clause

Chapter 9: Kuan Yin's Story 37

Chapter 10: Kuan Yin Today 40

PART THREE: Stay Wild, Wise and Free

Chapter 11: Stay Wild 43

Chapter 12: Stay Wise 47

Chapter 13: Stay Free 51

PART FOUR: The Feminine Advantage

Chapter 14: Evolutionary Advantages 56

Chapter 15: The New Wave of Research 60

PART FIVE: The Practice of Feminine Leadership
Chapter 16: Integrity and the Imposter Syndrome ... 65
Chapter 17: Characteristics of Feminine Leadership . 70
Chapter 18: The Future of Women in Business 74

PART SIX: The Eight Truths of Feminine Freedom
Chapter 19: Open Your Circuits 79
Chapter 20: Stay Wild 82
Chapter 21: Get Embodied 85
Chapter 22: Listen to Your Intuition 89
Chapter 23: Move Through Fear 91
Chapter 24: Find Your Sisterhood 95
Chapter 25: Lead Brilliantly 99
Chapter 26: Focus on What Matters 101

PART SEVEN: The Real Power of Positive Thinking
Chapter 27: What is Positivity? 104
Chapter 28: The Physiology of Happiness 106
Chapter 29: Pleasure Creates Profit 110

CLOSING: The Passing of the Warrior 113
About the Author 114

Preface

I recall a conversation over the summer of 2013, when a friend asked about the story behind my story—why did I love working with women? At that moment, I realized that I had carefully constructed a story—that was and remains true—but it was only the first half of the story. We'll come back to that in a moment.

The second half of the story: I had been a medical massage therapist and owned a clinic for a number of years. While I owned that business, I couldn't shake the deep calling to provide coaching and mentoring. After studying coaching for several years, I transitioned into coaching full time.

Coming out of the bodywork world and into the world of business was, to say the least, a culture shock. In the "real world" people don't tell you how wonderful you are every sixty minutes, like they do after you give them a massage! I felt lost, and at the same time I knew that I was supposed to work with small business owners. I had to reinvent myself, including the image of myself I presented to the world, and I molded myself into the standard business expectation: suit, sensible shoes, briefcase. I worked a lot with startup entrepreneurs to craft marketing strategies, hit sales goals, and use social media. It helped that I had, at one time, been both an insurance agent and a paralegal. So this world wasn't totally foreign. In a way, it just called for a costume change.

But costume change I did, and for ten years found success and satisfaction in that world. Until this year, when my friend asked The Big Question: What's the story behind why you work with women? I realized that I had to tell that story, and what was more, I had to let go of the carefully constructed ego offerings that seemed to compose my work.

Please don't misunderstand. I am really good at helping people grow their businesses. My clients typically double, if not triple their bottom line within three to four months of working with me. (It's the secret sauce of energy, intention, and inspired action, but that's a different story!)

I realized that I could help someone create strategies for growth and business development until we're both blue in the face, but if an internal transformation doesn't take place that allows and supports the change … guess what? NOTHING happens! Business growth is much more about who you BE than what you DO.

As I started to embrace this for myself, all of my deep seated fears began to come forward, and I entered that place of intense change and growth—the void. It's a creative place that brings new life and new directions, but while you're in it, frankly, it can suck … at least until you learn to ride it, play with it, and embody it.

I started to realize that the public face of what I had created was changing, and that the only thing I could really do was begin to show up in a new way.

My work as a coach has shifted this year from the DO to the BE. And that has emerged as a very feminine way of being in the world—allowing, not pushing. Being intentional and trusting that everything happens in perfection. Being IN the body, and not trying to leave the body with distractions, overwork, meditation or wine. Getting deeply connected and supported by my tribe of women. And empowering my clients to step into their wild, essential natures, to shed the bullshit and listen to the body.

I'm inspired by this story about Isadora Duncan. After dancing Tchaikovsky's *Marche Slave* in Boston, the free-thinking, unconventional dancer grabbed the red scarves attached to her costume and lifted them up, revealing her bare breasts to the audience, and prompting the mayor of Boston to ban any further performances from her. This book has been a dance that's been a long time in coming and reveals my truth in a way that I've never done before. As Isadora said to her Boston audience that night, "You were once wild here, don't let them tame you."

Part one of this story is the part that drives the feminine intention movement. And you'll read that later in this book. But for now, thank you for embracing your feminine intention. I love you and hold you in deep support.

Introduction

"The world is changed by your example and not by your opinions."
— Paulo Coelho

She showed up at my networking lunch looking polished and put together. Her hair was done up just right, her suit was fresh and pressed, her lipstick was conservative and her smile was bright and ready. But I could tell she was tired. As the lunch progressed, we became more comfortable with each other, and I learned what was behind that deep exhaustion I sensed.

Her day hadn't been any busier than usual. She'd gotten the kids ready for school, carted them off, then took herself to work. After our event, it was back to work (staying late to make up for the two-hour lunch), then off to pick up the kids from the sitter and cook an organic dinner. Of course, she would take a little time to look hot and sexy for her husband. She hoped she'd get to spend some time with him that night, but she had to work on the costumes for the kids' school play. Not once did she mention doing something for herself. Not once did she mention working on her small business, doing a hobby, or even going to a yoga class.

I see this all the time—women stretching themselves in different directions, trying to fit schedules and molds created by a masculine society. This mold looks nothing like women's natural shape. Much as the masculine-driven beauty industry has set high standards regarding physical appearance, the masculine-driven business and social worlds have created impossible standards for women, which devalue our inherent feminine qualities.

We're expected to behave like men at work (be assertive, close the deal, bring home the bacon), and like perfect mothers and wives at home (cook from scratch, go to all the kids functions, keep the house spotless). We're expected to keep rigid, masculine schedules, and to fit our femininity into clearly defined, segregated parameters. More and more, modern women just don't know what to do with themselves in a world where the masculine way of business and life has dominated for so long.

It shows up in a lot of ways. I see it in women who have started a business based on a very logical assessment of the market, and their potential profit. Their business might be successful, but it exhausts them and doesn't feed their passion. I see it in women whose fathers, mothers, husbands, teachers or friends have defined their talents—and thus, how they spend their days. I see it in women who know that they have to create an income, so they take a job they hate to pay the bills, while their dreams die slow deaths within them. But while it shows up in different ways, there's a common, underlying thread to all these women's stories: they're all filling limited roles, working hard to please others at the expense of their own growth and desires.

The woman at my event, like most of the women who come to me, was done trying to squeeze herself into this mold—done trying to work harder, go faster, do more, and defeat the competition in the name of the almighty dollar. In both the professional and personal spheres, women are ready to honor their natural qualities and step into their brilliance. This means changing—and challenging—everything.

But the work is worth it. As we stop settling for less, stop living for others, and start honoring who we are and what we want, we women are experiencing more happiness and success in our lives. And we're coming to understand that women are naturally better at business than men. Yes, you read that right! We're better at business! And it's those qualities that society has so long invalidated—like intuition, collaborative instinct, empathy and flexibility—which make us better.

Part One

The Seven Lies We Believed

"The feminine is not communicated by word or rite, but by presence and being."
— Robert Stein

There are seven key lies at the root of our attempts to fit these molds. These lies are such an integral part of our culture that we don't even realize they're in play. But we were raised on them—taught to believe them both explicitly and implicitly by our mothers, fathers, teachers, friends, and society at large. As you read through the next seven chapters, see if you recognize any of these mindsets at work in your life.

Chapter One:

The 1st Lie: Be Perfect

"Move into yourself. Move into your human unsuccess. Perfectionism rapes the soul."
— Marion Woodman

We come from a culture that values the best in everything. Valuing the best isn't a bad thing in itself, but when taken to extremes, it becomes toxic. It tells us that anything less than gold, anything with a minor flaw, isn't worth our time.

This includes us.

We're constantly striving for perfection. We work for the perfect body, a flawless performance at work, and the mother of the year award. We think that if we make a mistake, forget something, or fall short in any way, we're not deserving of rewards. These rewards could come in the form of love, appreciation, money, respect, a job, or anything we desire. Even little failures have big impacts on our self-image.

I see this a lot in women who own their own businesses, or work out of the home. They're obviously hard workers, and smart women—they've got drive, discipline, persistence, and vision. Often times, these women are also very interested in self-improvement, because they recognize that the principles and practices that make them happier, more satisfied people, will also make them happier, more satisfied at work, and as business owners. They understand that everything is connected.

However, these very qualities can often get women stuck at a particular point in their business. They get to a certain level of success, then spin their wheels and can't get any further. It's not that they're lacking vision, or persistence, or even a good plan. It's often that they're stuck on trying to make everything *just so* before they allow themselves to grow.

"If I could get this web page looking *just right* then I can be confident about contacting new prospects…"

"Once I get my eBook revised—again—I'll be able to move forward…"

"I really like this guy, but it feels like I have a lot of emotional baggage. I better go to therapy before I try a relationship…"

"I'd love to be a team leader, but I haven't finished my PhD yet…"

Each of these reasons not to move forward sounds very reasonable. After all, it's important to create high-quality business tools, and to be emotionally healthy in our relationships. But there's a point at which "reasons" become "excuses;" at which allowing our imperfections to prevent us from moving forward means we're stunting our own growth.

Know why? Because there's always going to be more we can improve about ourselves.

Self improvement is fantastic, and it's never complete. It should be a lifelong practice. But we mustn't confuse it with self perfection, or set some "self improvement finish line," after which we'll be ready to grow. With self-improvement, there is no finish line. Part of the wonder of life is that we can experience wild success and extravagant beauty even though we'll never have everything all figured out.

Many times, the best thing you can do is forge ahead despite imperfections. If you make a wrong decision or don't get the results you're after, you can always change your mind and adjust your course.

In his book, *Secrets of the Millionaire Mind*, T. Harv Eker has a great piece of advice for entrepreneurs, which you can use in any area of your life. He says:

"Ready, fire, aim!"

Eker means that we shouldn't spend too much time trying to set ourselves up for perfect success, because perfect success is never guaranteed. Instead, we should prepare ourselves as well as possible, then go for it! … and then, if we don't achieve our goal, we can take a step back and make adjustments.

We are human beings. We'll never be perfect, and we'll always make mistakes. We must forgive ourselves, remember that we are still worthy, and move on. Every time.

The lie in action:
Sara's launching her first online business, and she's excited. She's paid to have a website created, professional headshots taken, and crystal clear content written. She's been gearing up for this for a year, and she's finally ready. The week she launches, someone tells her that her site's colors and graphics are all askew in the Internet Explorer browser (although they look fine in all the other browsers—like Firefox, Safari, and Chrome). Explorer is a popular browser, and Sara's afraid that people who use it won't see her in her best light. She immediately takes down her site, and goes through a lengthy, technically-complicated process of sorting out every little kink so her site looks amazing in every browser.

Releasing the lie:
Despite the bad presentation in one web browser, Sara knows that's she's ready to launch her business, and she has something of value to offer. She's worked hard for this, and she's not about to back down because of a little technical difficulty. She puts a little caveat on her site, advising users that it looks best in Firefox, Safari, and Chrome, and begins the process of learning how to work things out for Internet Explorer.

Exercises:
Describe a situation where you tried to be perfect and failed. What was your most valuable learning from that?

Now consider a time when everything went as planned and you felt victorious. Hold the memory of that time in your mind, and close your eyes. Sit with it for several moments, and let it really sink into your being. Now say one word that describes this feeling state. This word will help you return to this feeling of power and success whenever you want.

Chapter Two

The 2nd Lie: Be Strong

"I can promise you that women working together—linked, informed and educated—can bring peace and prosperity to this forsaken planet."
— Isabel Allende

Have you ever felt reluctant to ask for help? Most women have. Many are even afraid to raise their voice for simple requests, like reaching up to a high shelf. They'd much rather go out of their way to hunt up a step-stool than ask someone taller (often a man) for help. (What will he think of her? Maybe he'll think she can't figure out how to reach a high shelf without him. Maybe he'll think she's incapable without his help …)

It's as though we believe that if we can't do something for ourselves, we shouldn't be doing it at all. We don't want to appear weak. These feelings often begin in childhood, when expressions of softness or vulnerability were chastised.

"Be strong" is a deeply-rooted sentiment in Western cultures, especially the United States. We value self-sufficiency and individuality. We value resourcefulness and the ability to rise above our circumstances to achieve. All these are good values. They're very empowering … but they're also very masculine values, and very destructive when taken to extremes.

We even strive to be perfectly strong in emotionally vulnerable areas. If we experience a deep disappointment, we're expected to keep a stiff upper lip and move on. If we lose a loved one, we're expected to grieve for a certain length of time, but not to break down at the office, and not to drag it out for too long. Emotion is equated with weakness.

While we value strength, it can lead to a lack of compassion toward those who don't accomplish as much, or who display their vulnerabilities. We see those who are vulnerable as not trying hard enough, focusing on the negative (and yes, vulnerability is seen as negative), and expecting others to do for them what they won't do for themselves.

This harkens back to Paleolithic hunter-gatherer times—when the Warrior ruled. If a member of the group wasn't strong, their weakness might slow down the entire group, making it harder to outrun predators or reach fruiting land in time to gather food.

And as for our individualism, we have every right to be proud of it. We have the right to be proud of who we are, and how resourceful we are when we can provide for ourselves. But we don't live in a vacuum. We live in a community, and communities function best when each member contributes and helps the others in some way. We serve as resources for one another. That's how we learn to value one another, our differences, and the unique gifts we bring to the table.

It's time to redefine strength.

Asking for help when we need it is a sign of strength. It means we're willing to rely on and trust others. It means we already know we're strong and we don't have to prove it. Honoring our emotions is also a strength. It means we are not afraid to feel or be vulnerable. It means we are deeply courageous, in a way those who avoid emotion are not.

Think about it. Do you know of any act of significance that has been accomplished by one person in complete isolation? I doubt it. In some way, there were other people involved.

Entrepreneurs are not exempt. Even if you are a one-person operation at the moment, you have customers you need to relate to, and as you become more successful, you will scale up to have employees or contractors.

It's important to understand how to work with people, so it's important to understand how people feel and think. We all have things in common like the need to feel important and appreciated, the hope for a better future, a need for direction, a need for encouragement, and a dream of success. Those are human qualities that all of us have. At the same time, we all want to feel unique in some way. The more authentic you are about these qualities in yourself and the more able you are to see them in others, the better you will connect with others.

If you can respect others and connect with them as well, you can inspire great loyalty. Think of five people you would go out of your way to help. I'll bet they all touched your heart in some way.

The lie in action:
Jennifer is a busy woman. She's a wife, a mother, and a full-time marketing professional. She's got enough on her schedule for two people. She'd like to ask her husband for help—maybe he could pick up the kids or make dinner several nights a week, so she could get some time to herself, to recharge. But she knows how much he values the few hours he gets to relax and enjoy the meal she's cooked, and she doesn't feel good about asking him to give that up. Instead, she ignores her feelings of overwhelm, telling herself it's just for awhile—until the kids are older. She tells herself this is the agreement she made when she decided to be a working mom and wife.

Releasing the lie:
Jennifer examines her schedule, and priorities the things that need to be done by her, specifically. Then she asks her husband to help with the other tasks, and to take care of the kids and dinner a few times a week. She knows this doesn't make her weaker—instead, it's making her family stronger. Instead of relying on Jennifer for everything, they all function as a unit. She even teaches her older

kids how to cook, and puts them in charge of dinner one night a week. Now, in addition to providing for her family, she's also empowering them (not to mention she finally gets some free time!).

Exercises:
Describe a situation where you knew you needed help, but didn't ask for it. What stopped you?

Put yourself back in that place mentally and emotionally, as much as you can. How does your body feel when you know you need help, but shy away from reaching out? What emotions come up, and what physical sensations can you detect?

What would have happened if you'd asked for help?

Sit with that scenario for awhile, and let your body feel how it would have been to receive help. What sensations arise for you?

Chapter Three

The 3rd Lie: Hurry Up

"The feminine takes time for spontaneity and slow time, honors inner reality, and gives values to feelings without brutally repressing them as 'sissy' or meaningless."
— Marion Woodman

Have you ever woken up with a sense of anxiety, as though you're already running late? Do you feel like there isn't enough time in your schedule to fit in everything important?

You've probably heard these phrases:

Time is money.

Be productive.

The early bird gets the worm.

Beat the clock.

The rat race.

You've got to move fast to get ahead.

Do more, be more.

These days, people are in a hurry regardless of what they're in a hurry about.

In the mid-20th century, many appliances were introduced and marketed to women to make their lives less complicated. A dishwasher, for example, would reduce the amount of time a woman spent at the sink, and then she'd have more time for herself. For most women, the reality turned out very differently. The dishwasher did reduce their time at the sink, but the resulting "free time" only filled with other tasks.

Why?

Part of it is personal, physiological habit. While we work, our brains produce associated hormones and emotions, and send those chemicals out to our cells. Our cells absorb these "work hormones," and get accustomed to them. It's like drinking the same cup of coffee every morning. You might not particularly like the taste of the coffee, but after a certain amount of time, your body begins to crave it, and your morning doesn't feel complete without it.

Just as we get addicted to things like caffeine and nicotine, our cells get addicted to the hormones and chemicals we feed them on a regular basis.

So if we work, work, work, our bodies adapt to that, and we begin to think of it as normal. Then when we find ourselves with free time, we feel like we're being lazy. We begin looking around for something else to take care of.

But our addiction to going fast is more than physiological. After all, if it weren't ingrained in our culture, we wouldn't adapt to it in the first place. It's a very masculine, production-oriented mindset, and it's all tied up with our economic structure and our values.

In many cases, capitalism finds more profit in creating more products, rather than in creating quality products. So instead of putting time, attention and craftsmanship into quality goods, we churn out as much as we can as fast as we can. Nevermind that we could charge more for quality goods—capitalism also conditions people to hold onto their money. We're all looking for a deal. Many people aren't interested in "shelling out the dough" for quality goods, when they can get something that looks the same but costs less.

And nevermind if they'll wind up paying more when their cut-rate product busts and needs repaired or replaced. In capitalism, we have no sense of the future. We live in a culture of instant gratification.

"Time is money" is really an oversimplification. Our addiction to the rush is really about *more*. The more we can do, the more we're valued by more people. So we strive to do more for our boss, our partner, our kids, our friends, our parents, our businesses, our clients, our employees. And sometimes we put stress on others to hurry up, so they won't throw a kink in our busy schedule and cause us to be late (to fail).

It's gotten to the point that it's no longer acceptable to do one thing at a time. We must be able to "multi-task." It's as though whatever we're doing is not as important as the next thing we're supposed to be doing.

The phrase "time is money" simply means that time can be turned into money. Well, this is true for just about anything we value. Time can be turned into love, for instance. It can be turned into playing music. It can be turned into conversation, education, or creating art.

Today, women are learning that doing something quicker does not mean doing it better. And it does not mean we're getting anything of value done.

There's a kind of backlash taking place against the drive to go, go, go. Slowing down, taking the time to appreciate life, and share with others is actually becoming marketable. People will pay for tea that takes a long time to brew. They'll schedule expensive retreats where their cell phones don't get reception. Studies are proving that multi-tasking is actually less effective than focusing on one thing at a time. Magazines like *Kinfolk* are eliminating advertisements that turn readers into nothing more than consumers, and are fostering a real sense of community, simplicity, and finding fulfillment in life.

This is what the rise of the feminine looks like.

The lie in action:
Cora's already handling several accounts at work. Her boss is impressed with her performance, and he asks her to take on another

account and get a big project done in one week. Cora thinks to herself, *One week? There's no way I can do that!* But she agrees. She wants to impress her boss, and she doesn't like telling people no. For the next week, she scrambles. All her other accounts suffer, she works late and misses date night with her boyfriend, but still doesn't manage to meet the deadline.

Releasing the lie:
Cora agrees to take on the new account on the condition that the deadline be set for two weeks instead of one. She appreciates her boss's high opinion, and knows the best way to keep that is by continuing to do her best quality work. She also values her quality of life—including her relationship with her boyfriend—and refuses to sacrifice that for her job.

Exercises:
The next time you find yourself rushing from one thing to the next, or you feel a sense of anxiety imploring you to hurry up, take a step back. What is it that you have to hurry up to accomplish? Will you fail to accomplish it if you slow down?

Schedule a half hour of your day in which you accomplish or do absolutely nothing. (No cheating at this!) Write about your experience during that half hour. Were you able to relax? Did you feel like you were being lazy, or avoiding responsibilities? Were you disappointing anyone during that time?

What did your body feel during that half hour? Tension in your belly? Jitters in your muscles? A calm warmth in your chest? There is no wrong answer to this.

The Feminine Intention – 13

Chapter Four

The 4th Lie: Try Harder

"Occasionally we will be overwhelmed, but mostly we will be enchanted."
— Jean Houston

This seems like a good sentiment at first glance. Of course, we should give everything in life our best shot, and we should never give up on something that's important to us. However, this lie goes hand-in-hand with "Be Perfect." So you cold-called 10 prospects. Could you have called 11?

You didn't have time to help with the kids' homework and cook dinner? Couldn't you have asked them quiz questions while you chopped vegetables and stirred sauce?

You didn't get the presentation done, even though you stayed late? Well, you were already working late—couldn't you have just stayed until the project was finished?

The answer to each of these questions is a reluctant, soul-sinking "yes." There is always more we can do. There's always an extra mile we can go. But if we are constantly straining ourselves to push harder in every way, on every front, we overextend ourselves and wind up depleted.

Trying harder all the time and seeing no results—or not enough results—means we're trying to force something to happen. It's a sign that we're not "in the flow;" not working in our brilliance. When we're living our purpose and doing the right thing, we feel great, and everything just seems to fall into place. We're infused with energy.

But if we keep pushing and pushing to make something happen, our energy is drained.

There's usually a misalignment of energy at work here. There's some part of us—some part of our heart, our mind, or our spirit—that's not one-hundred percent on board with what we say we want. Often, this misalignment is subconscious. We say we want something, and we push and push for it. We use empowering self-talk and gather support from friends and family. But we're not willing to step back and recognize the misalignment, or ask, "Why is this so hard?" Here are a few ways the Try Harder lie manifests:

A new saleswoman, who's gone through all the company training and believes fully in the product she's selling, but something in her just isn't comfortable trying to persuade others to do something. Something in her feels inauthentic. So she struggles with her work.

A woman who's been through a divorce and is looking for a new relationship. She dresses herself up to the nines and attends fun events with other singles, but she can't seem to attract and hold the interest of anyone she finds attractive. Something in her doesn't feel ready for a relationship yet, so she subconsciously withdraws.

Now, I'm not saying we should give up on our dreams if they take more than one or two tries to accomplish. Often, we just need to learn new skills, practice, or work out some energetic kinks before we can accomplish our goals.

But sometimes, it's healthier and more productive to step back and say, "Maybe this isn't working because it's the wrong thing for me." That can be hard to do. It takes real courage.

"When you get into a tight place and everything goes against you, till it seems you could not hang on a minute longer, never give up, for that is just the place and time that the tide will turn."
— Harriet Beecher Stowe

"If you have to ask for something more than once or twice, it wasn't yours in the first place."
— Madonna

The trick to trying harder, is knowing what it's important to try harder at. This means learning to prioritize (we'll talk more about priorities in the next chapter). It means sounding the depths of your heart and listening to the sensations of your body, to learn what's important to you. It means setting reasonable boundaries around the tasks you want to accomplish, and then just doing your best.

The lie in action:
Moriah's been happily married for eight years, but an uncomfortable distance has grown between her and her husband. When they get time together, conversations are like pulling teeth, and sex is just a memory. She's not happy anymore. But Moriah knows that you get out of something what you put into it, so she tries harder. She schedules more time to be with her husband, gets him to go to counseling with her, buys new lingerie, does her hair differently, and gets a boob job. But all she seems to be doing is making herself more miserable. Her husband isn't changing at all, and neither is her relationship.

Releasing the lie:
Moriah does what she can to reconnect with her husband and save her marriage, but she recognizes that no matter how much she puts into her relationship, she can't control her husband or his reactions. This is a two-way street. She puts a deadline on things, and tells her husband that if their relationship doesn't get better in three months, she'd like to separate. She's putting her "try harder" energy into something that's actually likely to yield results and happiness.

Exercises:

Write about an area in your life where you're trying and trying, but can't seem to make any progress. If nothing's coming to mind, write about a time in the past where you experienced this.

Sit with that situation in your mind, and pay attention to how your body feels. What sensations do you notice? How does it feel to be so stuck, physically and emotionally?

Oftentimes, what we're really trying for isn't obvious. If we're trying to make a sale, maybe we really want validation. If we're trying to save our relationship, maybe we really want to give and receive love. Ask yourself what you're really trying for. What's the "goal behind the goal" of your efforts?

Now allow your awareness to drop into your lower body and let yourself get really grounded and present. Feel your feet on the ground and notice the sensation of gravity pulling your feet to the floor. Let your breathing slow down and from this restful place, ask yourself, what one inspired action can you take towards this goal?

Chapter Five

The 5th Lie: Please Others

"A child can teach an adult three things: to be happy for no reason, to always be busy with something, and to know how to demand with all his might that which he desires."
— Paulo Coelho

For many of us, this is the Holy Grail of lies we've believed! Why do we try harder, hurry up and want to be perfect? To please others! We may say we have high standards for ourselves—and perhaps that's true. But where did those high standards come from? Most of the time, we've been taught to have high standards in order to please others.

But this lie goes deeper than that. It means that we don't know how to say "no" to others. We make other people's priorities our own, in order to get their approval.

We do it for our parents when we're children, because we naturally want our parents' approval, fearing we'd lose their love if we were "bad." We do it for our teachers in school, because they only want us to be successful; if we want to be successful, we'll recognize the teacher's priorities above our own. We do it for our bosses, because their priorities should be ours if we're going to be the best employee. We do it for our partners and children, because their needs should come before ours if we're going to be the best partner or mother. The list goes on and on.

This lie can be tricky, because there are plenty of commitments we really do need to uphold; plenty of promises we do need to keep. We have to go to work, or to that meeting with our client. We have to be at the soccer game we told our child we'd be at. Sometimes, we really do have to say yes to people.

But not all the time.

In the middle of all these necessary and not-so-necessary commitments, our own desires and priorities can get lost. We play so many roles for so many people, and work hard to live up to so many expectations, until one day we realize we have ignored our expectations for ourselves—our own desires. And these may be a complete turn-around from what everyone else wants from us. If we ignore them for long enough, they start to fester under our skin. We begin to feel resentment toward all those people and things we've said yes to, and our unhappiness weighs us down.

This is when we need to examine our priorities, to be sure we're spending our time on the right things.

Becoming more aware of our motivation for saying yes to people is also helpful. Sometimes we say yes to things because we feel pressured—either by the situation, or by another person. This "yes" comes from a place of fear, stress, or seeking approval.

Sometimes, we say yes because it's important to us to fill a certain role. This "yes" comes from a place of love and support.

We need to ask ourselves what the most important roles we play in life are. Are you a mother? A wife? A daughter? An employer? All your roles are important, but some are more so than others. Decide what the most important roles you play are.

Now, identify some of the most important things you do in each of those roles. Maybe as a wife, you make time for dinner with your husband, and put time into your appearance to look and feel sexy. Maybe as a mother, you make it to all your kids' school concerts— even if you have seven kids and they all have three shows a year. Maybe as an employer, you always pay your staff on time.

Understanding the most important things you do, in the most important roles you play, means you can begin to eliminate the non-essential tasks from your schedule. If the most important thing for you to do as a mother is to be at your kids' concerts, then maybe it's okay if you're not able to pick them up from school every day. If the most important thing you do for your marriage is eating dinner with your husband every day, then maybe it's okay if you can't make every company picnic with him.

This exercise can be a real breath of fresh air. Once you know your priorities, you don't have to bend over backward to accomplish things that aren't priority. You don't have to feel like you're failing anyone.

Then there's the part of you that's not nourished by being there for others, but needs to be nourished by self-care. We'll talk more about self-care and what it means in a later chapter, but for now, know that your success and happiness in all your other roles depends on identifying your most potent forms of self-care (not frivolous ones) and committing to them as surely as you commit to any other priority.

The lie in action:
Emily has a full schedule every week, and always schedules time for her job, her husband, and her kids, with enough left over to take care of meals and some housework. On Saturday, she has plans to get her haircut—it always makes her feel put together and sexy. But in the middle of the week, her daughter tells her about a last-minute bake sale the school's having on Saturday—of course, all the other moms are going to be there. Emily can't say no to her daughter's sweet excited eyes, so agrees to be at the bake sale, even though it means she won't be able to get her haircut for another two weeks.

Releasing the lie:
Emily acknowledges the need to be with and to support her daughter, and asks herself if there's a way she can do that while still getting her hair done. She clears her Saturday morning, and makes several dozen cookies from scratch with her daughter, just the two of them, before dropping her off at the bake sale and going to get her hair done. This

is called an integrity anchor, and is a way of anchoring a value-based action in daily life. An integrity anchor lets you make tough decisions with less guilt, knowing you've taken care of your most important relationships first.

Exercises:
Keep a list of everything you do in the day. Yes—everything! At the end of the day, sit down with your list, and write what your motivation was for doing each item. Did you do them for someone, or to fill a specific role? How many things did you do in order to avoid conflict? How many things have to be done by you, personally?

Think of a time when you failed to please someone. Maybe you didn't make a deadline, or had to cancel plans with your partner. Sit with the memory of that, and let it fill your body. How does it show up as a sensation, when you consider your own failure?

Consider what you really failed at that day. If you missed a deadline, did you fail to be reliable? If you canceled a romantic dinner, did you fail to show your partner how important they are to you? Get at the real root of why you feel inadequate.

What could you have done, or what could you still do, to accomplish your deeper motivations?

Chapter Six

The 6th Lie: I'm Not Good Enough

"If babies held the same tendency toward self-criticism as adults, they might never learn to walk or talk. Can you imagine infants stomping, 'Aarggh! Screwed up again!' Fortunately, babies are free of self-criticism. They just keep practicing."
— Dan Millman

One of the reasons we're always trying so hard—or, paradoxically, not trying at all—is because we believe we're not good enough. We're not perfect. We're not the best. We're just medium. And medium people don't win, so why even try?

We're good enough in some areas of life (and I stress good *enough*), but in others, we just can't get it together. We feel like we give 100%, trying harder all the time, but any progress we make is slow and small. Often, there's a quiet but persistent belief in the back of our minds that if somebody else were to try—somebody more worthy or intelligent—they'd probably succeed with very little trouble.

This lie comes into play when we compare ourselves to others … and we compare ourselves to others more often than we like to admit! It happens a lot on social media.

We may try not to compare ourselves to figures in the mainstream media. After all, those people are actresses and models, with teams dedicated to making them look good. We know those kids on the cereal commercial aren't actually that actress's children, and we know that fun, affectionate conversation has been written by professional storytellers.

Social media is different. Our contacts on Facebook are real people, most of whom we know. We see pictures of a colleague opening another branch of her business, and wonder what she's doing that we're not. We see pictures of a college friend running a marathon, and wonder why we don't have that self-discipline or motivation.

Suddenly, our own lives seem a little messy. We feel a little shabby and unaccomplished.

But don't be fooled. Most people put their best foot forward on social media. What you're getting there isn't the whole truth and nothing but the truth. It's carefully selected slices of the truth—the juiciest parts of the melon. Don't compare your average day to someone else's peak of success, or what I'll call their "airbrushed magazine moments."

Sometimes, not feeling good enough prevents us from reaching for our goals at all. I see this in women who have considered starting a business, or branching out with their current one, but have held back because they think they don't have what it takes to do a good job.

It's not that they don't have the intelligence. With a little dedication, they could pick up the skill sets and tools to develop their business. What they're really afraid of is that they're inherently not good enough to succeed. Sadly, their belief in their own limitations can impact their ability to learn, and set them up for failure.

The lie in action:
Robin's been working on a book for a long time, and thinks she's finally ready to self-publish. She has the book edited, but every time she sits down with it, she still comes across little mistakes here and there, and always notices things that can be improved upon. She revises repeatedly. One day, she sees her friend on Facebook has self-published a novel, and it's getting great reviews. When she thinks about her own book being critiqued and reviewed, she cringes inside. She just knows everyone will notice the little mistakes and ways it falls short. She decides not to publish.

Releasing the lie:
Robin knows that no work of art is ever perfect. She also knows that her book, despite its flaws, is probably better than she thinks, and has the potential to really touch people. Reasoning that if thousands of other authors can self-publish, then so can she, Robin goes ahead with her self-publishing plans.

Exercises:
Describe a time in your life when you accomplished something you previously believed to be impossible for you. Why had you thought you couldn't do it? How did it feel when you finally did?

Think back to that time when you believed you couldn't accomplish the above. Put yourself there as fully as possible, mentally and emotionally. How does that sense of limitation feel in your body? Where does it live?

Now remember how you felt when you accomplished that impossible thing. Again, sit with that memory. What emotions fill you up? See if you can sense where those emotions live in your body.

Create an Inspire File or Box, where you keep records of all the praise you get for the work you've done. This includes testimonials from clients, thank you notes, congratulatory notes, love letters, and anything else that makes you feel good about what you contribute to others.

Chapter Seven

The 7th Lie: Something's Wrong with Me

"I firmly believe that all human beings have access to extraordinary energies and powers. Judging from accounts of mystical experience, heightened creativity, or exceptional performance by athletes and artists, we harbor a greater life than we know."
— Jean Houston

This one is a deep core wounding that almost every woman—indeed, every adult—in North America suffers from. This lie is isolating and belittling. The essence of it is the belief that there must be something wrong with *you*, personally. You're probably broken in some way, or missing some piece that everyone else has.

This lie tells us there's a deep, fundamental flaw in us, rendering us incompetent and unsatisfactory. It tells us we're unlovable and we don't really matter—our feelings don't matter, our dreams don't matter, our knowledge and intuition don't matter.

At first glance, "Something's wrong with me," sounds a lot like, "I'm not good enough." It's deeply woven into all the other lies, as well.

You can think of this lie as the taproot of all the others. This is "the man behind the curtain." From an early age, we're told to do better. Try harder. Get better grades. Make better friends. Get a better job. A lot of this comes from our parents and teachers, and it seems to us that they want us to be something we're not.

That's why many of us grow up believing that we're supposed to be something we're not. If we could only change ourselves, then everything would be better.

Think back to when you were in school. There was probably at least one subject that you never quite "got." For many, it was math or English. Your grades were low no matter how hard you studied, and maybe your parents were always a little disappointed in this part of your performance. Why couldn't you just try harder and get better grades? It seemed very logical to them, and it was important if you were to get into a good college.

But you knew the truth. You would never be good in this subject. It wasn't a matter of trying, and it wasn't a matter of applying yourself. It was part of who you were. You hated this subject, and you suspected you would never use it after school.

You were probably right. Even if you're not in your ideal job, you probably don't work in a field that requires you to have skills that go entirely against your grain. Otherwise, you'd perform badly and lose your job.

This dynamic occurs in many areas of life—not only grades and school. It happens with desires, when we're told that we shouldn't want the things we want, or shouldn't enjoy the things we enjoy. We're told that we should do better and be perfect … but in order to do better and be perfect, we would have to be different people than we are. Therefore, we feel like there's something wrong with us.

The roots of this reach deep into our psyches. But the fruits manifest in different ways. We begin to think that we're not living up to expectations in many areas. Our abilities and our desires are flawed, and our failures are to blame for anything that goes wrong—or even *seems* to be wrong.

A woman may weave whole fantasies around her sense of inadequacy.

If her boss doesn't tell her she did a good job on the presentation, she thinks she must have messed it up terribly. Everyone is probably talking about the huge mistake she made that she's still unaware of, which will probably cost the company a big account.

If her husband fails to call home when he's running late, she thinks she's made him mad in some way, or forgotten something important (His birthday? His mom's birthday?). He's staying away from her because he's angry. Or what if he's having an affair with that co-worker he was talking about? Then she worries whether she's a sexy enough wife.

The sense that "something's wrong with me" is what's behind "imposter syndrome." Even after we begin to experience success and happiness in our lives, we secretly believe that we don't deserve it. We're fakes, and we hope nobody figures it out. (We'll talk more about imposter syndrome in a future chapter.)

Exercises:
Think of a time in your life when you were asked to learn a skill or accomplish a task, and found that no matter how much you tried to learn or applied yourself, you never lived up to expectations. Do you think that you could have accomplished this, if you had tried harder? Do you think that accomplishing this would have positively impacted your life in any way? Would it have been worth the effort?

Consider that situation when you were asked to do something you knew you couldn't. Sit with that memory, and let it fill you up. How does it feel in your body? Do you feel a sense of hollowness in your belly? Helplessness? Do you want to cry, or do you feel angry, with tension in your limbs? Do you feel numb? Whatever you experience, write it below.

What if your parents, teacher, boss, or whoever asked this impossible thing of you, told you that you didn't have to do it? What if they told you that they'd rather have you focus on the areas you excelled at? How would that feel, and what would those things be?

Think of a time when you wanted something that others said was wrong. Maybe it was a second slice of cake. Maybe you were attracted to someone you "shouldn't be" attracted to. How did it feel in your body to be told that your desires were wrong?

Write a response to the people who made you feel wrong for your desires. What do you wish you had said to them, or could say to them now?

Imagine a situation in which someone asks you to do something you know you're good at. How does it feel? How do you react? What is it that you're asked to do?

Chapter Eight

The Origins of the Seven Lies

"So why, if this is all so and too true, do women keep trying to bend and fold themselves into shapes that are not theirs? I must say, from years of clinical observation of this problem, that most of the time it is not because of deep-seated masochism or a malignant dedication to self-destruction or anything of that nature. More often, it is because the woman simply doesn't know any better. She is unmothered."
— Clarissa Pinkola Estes

So where did these limiting, destructive beliefs come from? Let's take a crash course in the history of the feminine!

First, we'll look at the arc of human history to see when these lies came into play. Then, we'll look at the life of an individual woman, and see when these lies become ingrained in her body, mind, and spirit.

There was a time in human history when societies were more matriarchal or matrilineal than today. Women were honored as tribal and cultural leaders. Gender equality was obvious to everyone, and even if some day-to-day tasks were divided up based on gender, there was no reason a woman couldn't be a warrior, or a man couldn't work in the home and do laundry.

Scholar Ruby Rohrlich, PhD, says that the earliest recorded societies in Sumeria left "more than a trace" of matriarchal values. In *Women in Transition*, she also wrote that "many scholars are convinced that Crete was a matriarchy, ruled by a queen-priestess."

There are also archeological records of goddess worshipping peoples across Europe. "Venus" figurines, with wide hips, big bellies and voluptuous breasts, have been discovered throughout Europe, and even in Siberia and Eurasia. These figurines date from the Upper Paleolithic era—that's about 50,000 to 40,000 years ago. Some are even older, dated to the Middle Paleolithic era. Venus figures and goddess images pop up throughout this period, and continue right on through the Neolithic era—that's the Stone Age.

Many scholars believe that while the societies that created Venus figures evolved, their descendants were still probably goddess-worshippers … until the Hellenes came along in the 3rd millennium BCE (the early Bronze Age).

The Hellenes—the early Greeks—honored a pantheon of gods and goddesses, but their supreme god was a sky god—like the god of Christianity. The Hellenes believed one strong god ruled over all, and that men were superior to women in many ways. Scholars speculate that when the Hellenes arrived in the Aegean, they oppressed the native goddess-worshippers, and imposed their own sky god cult on the people.

As Greek culture evolved, women lost much of their standing, freedom and respect in society. Athenian women were not even allowed to leave their homes, where they had to stay out of sight in a designated women's area—the *gynaikonitis*. The Ancient Romans adopted much of Greek culture, but Roman women had more freedom than their Athenian sisters. Even so, they weren't quite equal with men.

Now let's look at what was going on further north, in Scandinavia, Germany and the Celtic nations.

The Ancient Romans kept meticulous records of everything they did and encountered, and they recorded evidence of genderequal cultures. Tacitus, writing in the first century A.D. about the Germanic and Celtic tribes, noted that those cultures believed "there resides in women an element of holiness and prophecy, and so they

do not scorn to ask their advice or lightly disregard their replies … .
In the nations of the Sitones, woman is the ruling sex."

Respect for the feminine was especially strong in Germanic, Celtic, and Scandinavian cultures. Women were honored as equals, and it was widely understood that they had a more direct, intuitive connection to the gods, spirit, and even magic. This isn't to say that men couldn't be prophets; they certainly could, and there was no shame in a man being gifted in this traditionally feminine way. It wasn't "un-macho."

Women were allowed to own property, and had nearly as many rights as men. They weren't barred from the battlefield, if they wished to fight.

It's difficult to imagine some of these ancient women, our foremothers, believing they weren't good enough, or that they had to hurry up and accomplish more in order to be valued, or that they had to prove their worth to society by "being strong" and refusing help when they needed it.

As we know, the tide of history turned in the direction of patriarchy. It started with the Hellenes and the Romans, but it progressed with the Abrahamic religions.

The Abrahamic religions—Judaism, Islam and Christianity—were anomalies in the ancient world. Religions that focused on a single deity, a masculine sky god, to the exclusion of all others, were very different from the rest of the ancient world, where other societies recognized a bevy of gods and goddesses—male, female, animal and otherwise.

The Abrahamic religions were by nature patriarchal, and not very tolerant of other belief systems. You only need to look at the Old Testament to see that the early Hebrews were intent on conquering those who followed other gods.

Christianity soon emerged as the dominant religion in the Roman Empire. While Christ's message was one of equality, the early Christian church fathers believed women were inferior to men. They taught that women were by nature sinful, and were to blame for the original sin that damned the whole human race, and they looked down on any culture that valued women highly.

When Christianity and Rome came together, it was the perfect storm. These patriarchal beliefs spread all over Europe, facilitated by the structure and infrastructure of the Roman Empire. The Roman roads were particularly helpful, as was the influence of the army, and the administrative hierarchy the Romans created (the hierarchy of the Vatican echoes the hierarchy of ancient Rome).

It's from these patriarchal cultures that we see the seven lies coming into existence.

It's interesting to look at Scandinavian nations today. The Romans didn't manage to make it that far north. The people were too wild and the land was too rough even for the most disciplined, battle-hardened legionaries. So Roman influence and Christianity didn't make it to the Norse nations for a very long time. To this day, Christianity isn't as powerful a force in these nations as in the US, the UK, and Europe. In fact, nations like Denmark and Sweden are among the least religious in the world.

In his work "Society Without God," sociologist Phil Zuckerman writes about his research conducted with surveys, polls, and hundreds of conversations with Scandinavian people. Most didn't want to call themselves atheists, but were pretty uncomfortable and disinterested talking about religion at all. Zuckerman couldn't figure it out—was it a taboo issue?

Eventually, he came to the conclusion that religion wasn't a taboo issue. It was a *non*-issue. Most people just didn't care about it one way or the other.

By the way, the Scandinavian countries are among the most gender equal in the world, and they outperform the rest of the world when it comes to literacy, child welfare, education, economic equality, and overall life expectancy. Sweden offers 480 days of maternity leave and paternity leave, with pay, up until the child turns eight years old or finishes their first year of schooling. The days of parental leave can be distributed as the mother and father see fit.

Sound like a feminist policy to you? It does to me!

In the US, there is no nationally required term of maternity or paternity leave. Federal law allows for three months, but actual requirements vary from state to state. We're one of only eight nations that don't require parental leave.

"We stand with Suriname, Liberia, Palau, Papua New Guinea, Nauru, Western Samoa and Tonga in our assertion that we don't need to support new mothers in those weeks after they bring a child into the world."
— Dr. Claire McCarthy, pediatrician

There's certainly more at play here than whether or not Rome reached the lands of our ancestors, but it's a good indicator of what's going on.

During the 15th, 16th and 17th centuries, the witch-hunting craze was at its peak (although it actually began before the 1300s, and the last witches were burned after the 1600s). It swept through Europe, the UK and the US. Some estimates put the number of victims around 35,000, but biological anthropologist Greg Laden has said he wouldn't be surprised if the actual total was between 1 and 2 million. Between 75% and 85% of the victims were women.

The kind of scar such genocide and terror has left on the genetic memory of women is difficult to imagine. It's no wonder women learned to keep their heads down, obey authority, be invisible, and try to conform as much as possible. Anything that made a woman seem out of the ordinary, or which angered her husband, family or community, might attract unwanted attention. Anything from knowing about healing herbs, to curing illness with prayer, to arguing with her husband, to living in a community where a child had died could bring down an accusation of witchcraft. Displaying a strong intuition was certainly a no-no!

But over the course of centuries, science became more prominent. And with scientific understanding came the slow acknowledgment that belief in witchcraft was superstitious, and that women were not biologically inferior to men. (I'm not implying that intuition and healing are products of witchcraft. I'm simply saying that these skills were mysterious and unknown, and have been wisdom kept by women.)

This isn't to say that science acknowledged the power of the feminine. If anything, qualities like intuition and emotionalism were further disregarded. But the rise of science at least allowed women to begin stepping into the light and be acknowledged as intelligent in "a man's world."

However, playing in a man's world meant that women had to deny the parts of themselves society didn't value. If they didn't deny their intuition, suppress their emotional expression, and focus on their strength as individuals (instead of relying on the support of a community), men wouldn't take them seriously. So women strove to be strong, please everyone, and raced to produce as much as men and be equally valued by the economy (hurry up). As it happened, suppressing their femininity came pretty naturally by then.

Enter our mothers, grandmothers, and you and I.

Our mothers wanted us to be successful in this world. That's why they taught us to try harder all the time, to please everyone, and to be strong. We weren't taught to recognize and honor our intuition; we were taught to embrace logic. We weren't taught that vulnerability can be a strength; we were taught to hide it, and cover it up with shiny armor. And we were taught that the more masculine we could be, the less frivolous we would seem, and the more seriously we would be treated.

Modern research is beginning to show that our DNA actually remembers the experience of our ancestors. This means the traumas they felt, the beliefs they held, and the abilities they developed are literally coded into our genes. It also means that in addition to being taught to live the seven lies, the lies are actually coded into our DNA.

But research is also proving we have the ability to rewrite our own genetic code. More on this later!

Exercise:
Think about one of the lies that's particularly prominent in your life. Think about a specific circumstance in which it controlled you. Go into your body and feel that. Where does that lie live in your body?

Have you ever tried talking to your DNA? Try it now, when you sense that lie living in your body. Talk to your DNA, and ask why it wants to hold onto the lie. Tell your DNA that you trust it. You are grateful for what it's given you. But that it's allowed to let go now.

Imagine what it feels like to let go of the lie. Do you notice any differences in your body? How would your life change if you were no longer so invested in that lie?

Part Two
The Kuan Yin Clause

Chapter Nine

Kuan Yin

"You don't need to change the world. You need to change yourself."
— Don Miguel Ruiz

Kuan Yin is a Buddhist goddess of compassion, unconditional love and protection. She's one of the oldest and most venerated goddesses in the world, with her earliest recorded appearance coming from China in the 1st century. Today, her worship spans throughout Asia—including China, Japan, Malaysia, and Indonesia. She even has followers in Europe and the West.

The meaning of her name is "she who observes the mournful cries of all the world."

There are several legends surrounding her origin. One popular story says that her father planned to wed her to a wealthy but cruel husband. Kuan Yin tried to strike a deal with her father. She agreed to marry, so long as the marriage eased three misfortunes: She wanted her marriage to ease the suffering of people as they aged, when they fell ill, and the suffering surrounding death. She knew of a powerful healer who could create these miracles.

Her father was angry. He wanted her to marry a rich man, not a poor healer.

Kuan Yin wept and begged to be allowed to enter a temple as a nun instead. Her father agreed, but secretly told the monks to give her a brutal work regime—forcing her to hard labor day and night, so she would change her mind. She did the work in a spirit of service, and her kindness soon charmed everyone around her. Even the animals loved her, and helped with her work.

Her father became frustrated that she wasn't getting frustrated. He tried to burn down the temple, but Kuan Yin managed to put out the fire with the love in her bare hands. Now her father was really intimidated by his daughter, and he ordered her put to death. As the executioner strangled her, Kuan Yin forgave him for his lack of compassion, and she accepted his karmic guilt as her own.

Because she'd taken on his guilt, when she died she was taken to one of the hell realms, but instead of being tortured, she played music that lulled the demons, quenched the fire, and healed their pain. She turned the hell into a paradise.

Some legends have the demons sending her back to earth in a lotus flower, so they wouldn't lose their posts in hell!

Kuan Yin's stories take place in a world dominated by masculine energy. In them we see the divine feminine willing to subjugate herself to the masculine, if it will bring about some greater good. We see the masculine afraid of her gentle strength and power. We also see her taking on the masculine's sins as her own—her story is full of the feminine being responsible for, and suffering for, the sins of the masculine.

Multiple stories focus on her and her father. In one, her father was blind, and she came to him disguised, to convert him to the path of Buddhism—which is famous for its dedication to compassion, widely recognized as a feminine trait. She told her father that if he ate one of his children's eyes, he would see again. But none of his children were willing to give up their eyes. Kuan Yin, the future goddess, gave her own eye to her father.

Another version of this story says the only cure for her father's illness was a medicine made from the eyes and hands of someone who had never felt anger. Kuan Yin immediately gave up her own eyes and hands.

Symbolism is everywhere in these old legends. One interpretation of these "healing eyes and hands" stories is that when Kuan Yin sought to heal her father and convert him to Buddhism, this symbolizes the embodiment of the feminine trying to teach the patriarchy to open its eyes and develop compassion.

Her father needed to see with fresh eyes, and to have hands that were more compassionate. Only then would he be healed.

But the children of the patriarchy couldn't help with that—they were raised in exactly the same way! They would experience anger in the same way, see the world in the same way, and would be on the path to developing the same blindness and sickness as their father.

Kuan Yin's vision, grace, mercy and compassion were the only intervention that could cure the world's suffering.

Chapter Ten

Kuan Yin Today

"I will no longer allow anyone to manipulate my mind and control my life in the name of love."
— Don Miguel Ruiz

Kuan Yin could be described as a bodhisattva—an enlightened being who loves the world so deeply, that she has vowed not to enter Nirvana, but to remain on earth as pure spirit and energy, until every soul in the world that cries out for help has been healed and enlightened.

Many women can relate to Kuan Yin's desire to protect, guide and support other beings. Nurturing others is a feminine quality. Another feminine quality is patience—like Kuan Yin, we want to wait for those we love to find their own way, providing help and protection when they need it.

We have the belief—whether it's conscious or subconscious—that if we move ahead on our own journey, we'll be neglecting people we love, or leaving them behind. We feel we have to keep the peace, and continue playing the role of attentive wife/mother/daughter/employee, because otherwise we might make our husband/kids/parents/boss mad. But even though we feel loyal and protective toward those we love, we shouldn't play small for them.

Kuan Yin is a goddess of compassion. The meaning of compassion is "suffering with." Many women seem to believe that by suffering with an unsatisfying situation, or with someone else's demands, they're contributing to the greater good.

But suffering for the greater good doesn't actually do any good. In fact, it does the opposite of good.

Imagine if Kuan Yin had allowed herself to suffer just to keep her father happy, and didn't let her brilliance shine. The goddess didn't act to please others' shortsighted versions of happiness. Like a lotus growing out of the mud to bloom on the surface of the water, she turned her suffering into beauty.

Let's look at another example of "suffering for the greater good."

In the days of slavery, a woman slave's job was to please her masters—whatever that required. If she did as she was told and did her job well, hopefully everything ran a little smoother and nobody got mad at her! However, making sure things ran smoothly on the plantation did nothing to elevate the world out of its slumber of inequality.

These days, we're not slaves. But we're not completely free either. Wayne Dyer says, "Freedom means you are unobstructed in living your life as you choose. Anything less is a form of slavery." Though we've come a long way on the path to freedom, we still have a long way to go.

We have the responsibility to demand our freedom and our brilliance. To stop disappearing behind the needs of others. Freedom is never just handed to us. It's always something to be fought and won. When we commit to being wild, wise and free, we not only liberate ourselves to live our brilliance—we inspire our friends and pave the way for our daughters. That's when we really emulate Kuan Yin; we work toward our own enlightenment before sacrificing ourselves for others.

Part Three

Stay Wild, Wise and Free

Chapter Eleven

Stay Wild

Wild: *adjective.* Living in a state of nature; undomesticated; uninhabited; natural; unadulterated

"Living by principles is not living your own life. It is easier to try to be better than you are than to be who you are."
— Marion Woodman

Women everywhere are noticing one or more of the seven lies at work in their lives. Even if she hasn't read a list like the one above, a woman might get an unshakeable sense that something is wrong—and it's not wrong with her. "I shouldn't feel so rushed all the time," she might say. "Life isn't supposed to be about jumping left and right to please everyone." Or, "I know I've got a great business and I'm doing everything I'm supposed to. Why can't I make it work?"

After realizing her unhappiness isn't going anywhere, she makes the declaration, "There's got to be a better way!" It's the moment of truth, the big "Hell no, I'm not doing this anymore!"

Those are wild words. They mark the beginning of our freedom, when we start the process of undomesticating ourselves, and determine to embrace our natural talents and honor our needs—no matter what. This is a journey to our own brilliance. This is the beginning.

Choosing to live in alignment with our talents and desires means expressing our brilliance to the world. It means identifying our most potent forms of self-care, and making them a priority. It means stepping away from situations, relationships or jobs that don't feel right for us, and refusing to rent out our time, energy, and mental space to the priorities of others.

We're not always sure what's going to fill that time and mental space once it's uninhabited, but we know that it's got to be better than what we've been doing. Somehow we intuitively know that there is more joy, satisfaction and happiness behind that unopened door.

Sometimes, when we realize we have to make a change, we can get stuck in a loop of guilt and negativity, blaming ourselves for creating an unsatisfying life in the first place. Don't fall for this! There were hundreds, if not thousands, of factors that led us to accept unhappiness as a way of life. We've explored seven in depth in the first part of this book. Most of these influenced us when we were too young and unaware to know what was happening.

We didn't choose to be taught that we're not good enough. Neither did our parents consciously choose to drum that lesson into our minds. It just happened, and we adapted to survive. We trained ourselves to live in spite of negative circumstances, fighting like brave soldiers through the daily battle of our lives.

Be compassionate towards yourself. Judging yourself will only waste precious energy. And that's energy that you can put to better use—because just as we trained ourselves to be unhappy, we can train ourselves to be happy.

Because now we're conscious women. Now we have the power to look around, determine what needs to be changed, and change it. Do you see why that's a wild action, in the "civilized" culture that domesticated us for different things?

Not a lot of women venture into the wild—it's unknown territory. Most women stay tamed, and continue to do, be, and act in ways that won't offend anyone or cause a stir. Being tame is safer, they understand the rules, and it's what everyone expects of them. The seven lies their mothers believed rest heavily on their shoulders.

But going wild doesn't mean going crazy. It isn't selfish, reckless or impulsive. It's simply connecting with and expressing our natural state. And it's from this place that our natural brilliance arises. Our natural brilliance is the passion and purpose that lives in our bones and drives our dreams. It's the honest expression of our most sacred emotions.

So how do we find our brilliance? Choosing to be wild and acknowledging our dreams is part of it—but we must also acknowledge our past.

Exercises:
Write about a time in your life when you felt purely happy. It can be an isolated incident, a span of years, or perhaps a certain place in childhood you associate with being carefree and joyful. As you write, be sure to include the emotions you experienced, and what inspired them.

What makes you feel happy today? Are there particular activities, hobbies, or circumstances that come to mind? Is it your children's smiles? Write the emotions that come up when you think of what makes you happy today. (For instance, if your daughter's smile makes you happy, why? Is it because you want her to be safe and happy herself, and thinking that she is makes you feel like a good mother?)

Take a look at the emotions you wrote down above, and what inspired them. Are there other activities you could do that would inspire the same emotions?

The Feminine Intention – 45

What makes you feel special? Is there a talent you have that makes you feel exceptional? Does getting pampered at a day spa make you feel like a princess? Does helping others make you feel like you're fulfilling your purpose? There are no wrong answers here, and you're not writing a manifesto for your life goals. Just write how you like to feel special.

What would you do if you knew your success was guaranteed? Why would you do that thing? What's stopping you from doing that thing now?

Chapter Twelve

Stay Wise

"When a creature is exposed to violence, it will tend to adapt to that disturbance, so that when the violence ceases or the creature is allowed its freedom, the healthy instinct to flee is hugely diminished, and the creature stays put instead."
— Clarissa Pinkola Estes

Many women have cherished the same unrealized dreams since they were children. Others aren't quite sure what their passion is. In both cases, there's uncertainty about what we have to offer the world, and whether we're worthy enough to offer it. We don't believe in our brilliance.

Getting wild can certainly help. But it's also important to get in touch with your past, and what may be holding you back. Your past holds the source of the pain that's been dulling your brilliance.

Perhaps this is something that's been hurting you for a long time. Maybe it hurt you in the past, or maybe it's an ongoing, chronic condition. This is your deep wound. Every woman has one. It's not that every woman has experienced acute trauma —although some of us certainly have. Sometimes your deep wound forms year after year as you work a job that kills your soul. Sometimes it's a self-betrayal you experienced as a young woman, before you understood what was really true and important for you.

When we experience trauma, our bodies go into "fight or flight" mode. Surges of adrenaline and cortisol pump through our systems, preparing us to handle the traumatic situation by fighting back or running away. This is easily illustrated in situations where we're threatened by an external force—like being approached by a mugger.

The term "fight or flight" should actually be "fight, flight or freeze." Because if we don't fight, and we don't flee, another response to threats is to simply go still—we become unable to move, unable to react, protect ourselves, think clearly, or run for safety. We feel helpless, small, and threatened, but we can do nothing except endure what's happening.

Let's look at an example. When a deer is hit by a car and collapses, it often doesn't move for several moments. This is because its system doesn't differentiate between being hit by a car, and being attacked by a predator. Its body is flooded with hormones, preparing it to be eaten—it's gone rigid and numb, to mitigate the pain of death … even though the car isn't going to eat it.

This happens to us, too. When we can't fight, and we can't run, we freeze and ride out the threat. Our bodies are still filled with stress hormones—adrenaline and cortisol—we're just not doing anything about it. The "freeze" response is common, but it leaves you with no way to discharge the energy of trauma from your body. You try to forget about what happened, but your body internalizes this energy and stores it for recall later. It forms a "blueprint" for how to respond to stress.

Women can experience the "freeze" response to immediate danger, acute trauma, and slow soul-killing chronic problems.

We actually experience "freeze" more often than "fight or flight." Think about it—if you're approached by a mugger you'll most likely freeze, and your body records that experience; you remember it in your muscles and bones. But if you fight back, your body records that experience, too. The same goes if you flee from the mugger.

But later, when your body calls up the experience (and it will, whether you want it to or not), it can't fight or flee. The mugger's not there; there is no immediate threat. So you're just forced to re-experience the negative emotions, feeling helpless in the grip of fear.

Our bodies learn to respond to pain and discomfort, again and again, by going still, allowing it to happen, and waiting for it to be over.

So we come to believe that helplessness and unhappiness is the only possible response to trauma and discomfort. We learn to endure, because we've never learned that it's possible to change our response.

But it is very possible to change our response, and create a different reality—one where discomfort, fear and helplessness are transformed into pleasure, confidence and possibility.

It takes courage and intention, but it's worth it.

The first thing to do is identify your deep wounding. Whether you experienced something like abuse as a child, a traumatic divorce, or constant creative rejection, you must recognize and face the source of your pain. Only then can you transform it. Your deep wounding creates wisdom. Within the wound is a compass that can guide you toward healing, and toward expressing your brilliance in the world.

Oprah Winfrey suffered sexual abuse as a child, and decided to spend her life empowering and connecting women. She never wanted anyone else to go through the isolation and powerless she had gone through.

Sonia Sotomayor was diagnosed with diabetes when she was seven. Fearing that she would die young, and unwilling to rely on the undependable adults in her life, she developed a fierce sense of independence and desire to achieve that helped her rise above her circumstances to become the first Latina woman on the United States Supreme Court.

Each woman's determination to heal her deep wound led her to serve and inspire millions of others.

My own story is an example of this. When I was 18 years old, right out of high school, I got married and joined a restrictive religion with severe rules for women. I was forbidden to watch TV or listen to music. I was forbidden to get my haircut or wear pants in public. And in the name of religion, my husband regularly intimidated and abused me, both mentally and physically.

I endured for seven years. When I finally worked up the courage to approach church leaders about the abuse, I was turned out by the congregation and my family. I had no money, no education beyond high school, and no community. But I had three daughters, and I was determined to make a new life for us in the world.

The only thing I knew how to do was clean houses, so I started a housecleaning business. I knew that my family's success depended on my own, so I poured every extra cent and spare minute into learning. I earned certification as a paralegal, then as a massage therapist. Finally, I started a massage business, which I ran for eighteen years.

In time, I had two more daughters, then remarried an amazing man and gained two wonderful stepdaughters. I am now mother to seven beautiful, inspiring women.

I'm called to do the work of empowering women by the experiences of my past, and the many women in my life, including

my daughters, who surround me every day. Healing my own deep wound has been a blessing with far-reaching results, helping me to inspire others as they claim their own freedom and create their own destinies. I feel so honored to do this work.

That's the feeling we all get when we're living our brilliance. I deeply hope you are able to experience it.

Listen to your own deep wounding; don't hide from it. The wound itself will tell you how to heal it, and what you can bring to the world.

Chapter Thirteen

Stay Free

"Whenever you become empowered, you will be tested."
— Caroline Myss

Living our brilliance requires that we create our freedom. There are many people invested in keeping us tamed and obedient —in foisting their own priorities on us. There's work involved in committing to our wisdom and our purpose, and it takes real courage to be wild, to navigate the unknown in a way that makes us feel good. There may be some experimentation at first, as we learn what form of self-care is most nourishing, and how to work our passions into our daily lives.

Freedom is a universal human desire, the deep need to create the time and space to embrace the values and actions that satisfy us the most. Freedom is the inherent right of all people, not just women. It means finding a way to express our deepest thoughts and resulting actions, to stop hiding from ourselves. It was, after all, just a little over one hundred years ago that women were unable to vote in the United States.

Often, we find we need to create freedom in more than one area of our lives. Why is this? Because the way you do anything is the way you do everything.

It's not because we're governed by dominant circumstances. It's because we're governed by dominant habits and emotions. These habits and emotions are usually set in place when we're children, and are usually centered around the seven lies.

That's why when we seek freedom in one area of our lives, we're more than likely seeking it in several. We're not looking to change a single external situation, like a low balance in our bank account, or an unfulfilling relationship. We're looking for a new way to embrace our lives; a new sense of freedom and liberation that comes from deep within—and which leads to the ability to change our circumstances as we see fit, to create a life that reflects our deepest desires.

That's what finding our brilliance is all about. So how do we get there?

The first step is awareness. Simply become aware of what's working and what's not working in your life. What makes you feel passionate? What makes you feel wild, wise and free? Pay attention to your feelings—your emotional reactions to your daily schedule, and the desires that crop up in those quiet moments between tasks. *I wish I could go sailing right now*, or *I wish I could tell my boss how I really feel*. Pay attention to moments of jealousy, too—jealousy can be a powerful indicator of our deepest dreams. If you're envious of your friend the actress, perhaps this is a call for you to get involved in theater. Also, pay attention to the thoughts and memories that cause you the most pain. These are indicators of your deep wound.

When you make a habit of being aware of your feelings and desires, you're getting in touch with your wisdom. You'll soon know what makes you feel wild and free, and as you commit to doing more of that, you move into your brilliance.

Another important step toward freedom is forgiveness.

Forgiveness is especially important in light of your deep wounding. A lot of women resist forgiveness. They see it as letting someone (either another person, or themselves) off the hook.

Would you believe it if I told you that forgiveness isn't about dismissing guilt? It's not about pretending a painful experience didn't happen. It's about allowing yourself to release the negative emotions you've been carrying around, and moving on with your life.

Think you don't have what it takes to come to a place of forgiveness in your heart? It's true that forgiveness is often a process that can take time, but it's also true that every human heart is capable of deep, wild, powerful forgiveness.

"Forgiveness is nothing more, and nothing less, than an act of self-healing."
— Eva Mozes Kor

Eva Mozes Kor was one of the well-known "Mengele twins," who was subjected to medical experimentation at Auschwitz. Eva survived the Holocaust, and the film *Forgiving Dr. Mengele* tells the story of her journey from pain, rage and anger, to forgiveness and healing.

"Just to be free from the Nazis, that did not remove the pain they had inflicted upon me. There might be another way that survivors can heal themselves. I have found one way: forgive your worst enemy. It will heal your soul, and it will set you free."

Eva didn't restrict her advice to situations as traumatic as the Holocaust. Suffering is universal, and forgiveness can be applied to any situation—from a road-rage encounter to a loveless marriage to a Holocaust.

"Victims of every type of situation always feel hurt, angry, hopeless, helpless and powerless. And I discovered at that other end that I had tremendous powers … I had the power to forgive the god of Auschwitz … No one could give me that power, and no one could take it away. That really made me feel very good inside."

One day, Eva stood side by side with a former Nazi doctor in Auschwitz itself, and she read a declaration of forgiveness for all the Nazis involved in the slaughter and oppression of her, her family, and her people. Later, when she talked about signing that declaration, she said, "I immediately felt that a burden of pain was lifted from my shoulders. That I was no longer a victim of Auschwitz. I was no longer a prisoner of my tragic past. I was finally free. The day I forgave the Nazis … I also forgave myself."

If you can access your heart's powers of forgiveness, you can allow yourself to step away from the pain that keeps you from moving forward in your life. You develop the power to transform that pain into a liberating experience for yourself, and for any others your life's purpose affects. Your brilliance will shine on the world around you.

Awareness of what allows you to shine, and forgiveness of the forces that have kept you in the darkness, will be your great allies on your path to freedom. They'll help you implement healthy habits, and release negative and destructive emotions.

In the beginning—and sometimes even after you're living your brilliance—you'll often find yourself looping back into old patterns of thought. Those seven old lies will rear their heads and have you thinking,

"I've got to take care of people!"

"I have to do this faster!"

"I'm not good enough for this."

But freedom is always worth fighting for. Stay your course.

"Forgiveness is a mystical act, not a reasonable one."
— Caroline Myss

Part Four

The Feminine Advantage

When we talk about feminine qualities giving women a natural advantage in the workplace or in our personal lives, what qualities are we referring to? And can we really classify them as "feminine" in such a sweeping way?

We can, actually. In The Athena Doctrine, authors John Gerzema and Michael D'Antonio conducted research in over 30 countries to determine the qualities people consider feminine, and those they typically consider masculine. The results were astounding. Not only do people across cultures have common interpretations of "feminine" and "masculine" traits—they also overwhelmingly agree that the world would be a better place if feminine qualities were more highly valued, and if men in power thought more like women.

Masculine Qualities	Feminine Qualities
Strong	Compassion
Logical	Intuition
Self-Reliance	Cooperation
Brave	Listening
Overbearing	Free Spirited
Assertive	Expressive
Rigid	Socially Responsible

The Athena Doctrine tells us the world is ready for a shift in values from the masculine to the feminine.

Chapter Fourteen

Evolutionary Advantages

"We are reluctant to live outside tribal rules because we are afraid of getting kicked out of the tribe."
 — Caroline Myss

It's true that men and women both have masculine and feminine traits. However, each gender evolved with emphasis on a certain set of characteristics. Men's and women's brains are just wired differently.

Many thousands of years ago, during the Paleolithic era, men used their natural skills for the hunt, the chase, the attack and the kill to bring meat to the community. They evolved to think in terms of clannishness, an "us vs. them" mentality. Meanwhile, women remained behind, making use of their own natural skills to gather food, care for children, cultivate community—a "we're all in this together" mentality—and defend the camp.

Women would talk to each other, help each other gather food, and help each other raise the children. It was important for survival to work together and forge a strong sense of community, so we evolved to collaborate with and care for one another. This ability to gather sustenance through a spirit of cooperation makes us natural leaders, and more effective leaders than men.

It's not unnatural for the masculine mind to devalue what it perceives as weak. It was a necessary evolved trait in tribal hunting culture. A weak hunter could put the whole party in danger; it could mean the hunting party missed a kill, and the entire tribe went hungry.

There's a subtle difference in the way men and women think of social groups, too. Men evolved to think in terms of "clan," and women in terms of "community." Men were hunters and warriors. They developed a keen sense of protectiveness for their women, children and clan. They had to be brutal towards opposing clans if they were going to defend their own.

While they worked together on hunts, the success of the hunt required silence. Men didn't chatter to each other while closing in on prey.

Women evolved to think of their group more as a community. Gathering food, raising children, caring for the elderly, and creating goods (like clothing and tools) was conducive to conversation, so women chattered to and learned from one another while they worked.

This demonstrates another key difference between male and female brains. Men's brains evolved to focus on one thing at a time. Women's brains evolved to encompass many things at once.

Also, the language and communication parts of our brains are different. In general, men's language skills are housed in one side of the brain, while women's are distributed more evenly throughout the entire brain.

Researchers have found that among victims who've experienced trauma to only one side of their brain, men tend to lose more of the functions associated with that hemisphere than women do. This suggests that those functions are spread more uniformly throughout the woman's brain, while in the man's they're more centered in one hemisphere.

I'm going to use a stereotypical situation here, to demonstrate. A woman and her husband host a football party, with several other families attending. While the men cluster around the flatscreen, grunting and yelling at the TV, and rooting for their clan

(team) to "kill the other guys," the women spend a little time in the kitchen, preparing food, having more detailed conversations, and tending to the children. (Isn't it interesting that even though the kids may be playing on their own, if one of them needs something, they'll usually have the instinct to go to mom in the kitchen rather than dad, who's focused on the game? Children can tell which parent is more likely to have the attention they need.)

Our brain wiring makes us better able to organize and keep track of multiple things. It also means we're more attentive to the world around us, and more "open," which can contribute to intuition. This is especially helpful in the business world, when we must balance employees, clients, payroll, marketing, meetings, and all the other things that contribute to a successful company. Not to mention our relationships, our health, our hobbies, our homes, and all the other things that contribute to a successful, happy life!

Feminine qualities have traditionally been devalued and degraded by masculine culture, which admires strength and believes the seven lies. In the business world, "closing the deal" and "making a killing" are valued over personal relationships and integrity. That's why women, especially in business, have felt pressured to work in ways that made them uncomfortable—to sacrifice their needs and talents, their integrity, and their compassion.

However, society is evolving. We no longer need to depend on a hunter-warrior culture for survival. We have moved from an industrial, to an information-based and now to a knowledge-based society. A knowledge society promotes human rights and offers equal, inclusive, and universal access to all knowledge created. The UNESCO World Report establishes four principles that are essential for development of an equitable knowledge society:

Cultural diversity

Equal access to education

Universal access to information (in the public domain)

Freedom of expression

Women naturally create collaborative, knowledge societies, and are coming to realize that when we embrace our feminine qualities, instead of trying to ignore or suppress them, they give us a strong advantage. Playing the game our way makes us much stronger teammates than trying to play the masculine way.

It truly has the power to transform the world from a bunch of opposing clans, into a collective of cooperative individuals.

Chapter Fifteen

The New Wave Of Research

"If it is not tempered by compassion and empathy, reason can lead men and women into a moral void."
— Karen Armstrong

Let's talk a little more about some of the new research being done in books like *The Athena Doctrine*.

Gerzema and D'Antonio, the authors of *The Athena Doctrine*, conducted a number of global surveys, but their two main studies were done with separate groups. One group was asked about various personality traits and qualities, which they had to designate as "masculine," "feminine," or "neither." Another group was given a list of those traits, and asked whether they would contribute to a more fair, happier world.

Here are a few qualities people across cultures consider feminine. Can you see how valuable these traits are in a leader?

Expressive — A leader who expresses her mind and her emotions can put people at ease, since they don't have to play guessing games about what she's feeling. Her emotions can also inspire those on her team.

Flexible — The ability to go with the flow and get things done, even if one of her key employees has to leave a project for personal reasons. Being flexible also means she's open to ideas other than her own.

Reasonable — She doesn't send her team into a frenzy making impossible demands, and she can listen and understand other points of view.

Intuitive — She senses what is right for her company, and understands how her team feels. She often knows what the right thing to do is, even if it doesn't seem logical.

Patient — She knows that time is on her side, not an enemy.

Kind — Having a keen imagination, she values treating others as she likes to be treated. She cares deeply for the human element in business, and in the world.

Integrity — She does the right thing, even if it means she'll lose money. Her opinion of herself, and her reputation as a woman, is worth more to her than dollar signs.

Passionate — She gives herself fully to ideas that get her energy pumping. She knows that if she's passionate about something, there's a whole group of people who share her feelings (such as clients or employees).

Protective — She's not willing to expose others to attacks, and she wants to make sure people are comfortable.

Transparent — She communicates clearly, and doesn't hide her motivations in order to manipulate people.

Collaborative — She values working together toward a common goal, rather than issuing orders from on high and expecting people to jump at her word.

Supportive — She helps those who don't understand, is flexible for those who need different arrangements, and expresses appreciation and encouragement often.

Intelligent — She's smart in more ways than one. She's educated, but also has common sense and emotional intelligence. This means she takes different kinds of information into account when making a decision.

"People question whether there's too much power in the hands of businesses and institutions. People worry about basic fairness."
— John Gerzema

In Gerzema and D'Antonio's surveys of over 13 countries, including the US, UK, Canada, Japan, India, China, and Mexico, the majority of people claimed to be dissatisfied with the conduct of men. Overall, people who were dissatisfied included 54% of men, and 57% of adults. In the US, two-thirds of people agreed. And in Japan and South Korea, a full 79% of people said they were very disappointed in the conduct of men in their countries, especially men in positions of power.

Asking a slightly different question—"Would the world be a better place if men thought more like women?"—survey responders agreed in even higher ratios. 63% of men across the world agreed, including 79% of men in Japan, 75% of adults in France and Brazil, and 72% of people in the UK.

The groups with the lowest opinions of masculine behavior, and the highest opinions of feminine values, were usually young people, including millennials.

Faith Popcorn is an author, futurist, and the CEO of BrainReserve, a marketing consulting firm famous for predicting future trends. Popcorn has accurately predicted trends like the rise in home delivery services, and the demand for more fresh food. She was even hired by the USPS when they wanted to know what the future of stamps would be.

In 2009, one of her predictions for the near-distant future was the trend of what she called, "cashing out"—when working adults look around at their busy, complicated lives, question their happiness and social impact, and "cash out" to opt for more simpler living. We're definitely seeing that now, with magazines like *Simple Living* present in every grocery store aisle, and magazines like *Kinfolk* eliminating advertisements from their pages and subsisting on subscriber fees alone.

Popcorn has also predicted that feminine values would become more important in business. She referred to it as the "EVEolution," and said, "The way women think and behave is impacting business, causing a marketing shift away from a hierarchical model, to a more relational one."

Millennia of evolution, years of anthropological research, and current studies agree: the feminine's time to lead has come. Even men are crying out for a more feminine approach to organizing society, relating to one another, and running business.

Part Five

The Practice of Feminine Leadership

Chapter Sixteen

Integrity and Imposter Syndrome

"I no longer agree to treat myself with disrespect. Every time a self-critical thought comes to mind, I will forgive the Judge and follow this comment with words of praise, self-acceptance, and love."
— Don Miguel Ruiz

Feminine leadership looks different than the masculine brand the world has known for so long. All the strongest feminine traits come together to create the picture of a dynamic team builder who leads by inspiration, cooperation and encouragement, and who values relationships and integrity as much or more than the bottom line.

We'll address some particular characteristics of feminine leadership, and how to express those, in the next chapter. For now, let's talk about one of the main challenges women often encounter in positions of power, leadership, or success.

"I feel like a fake."

"I'm not sure I deserve all of this."

"I keep waiting for somebody to figure out that I shouldn't be here."

This is what we call "imposter syndrome." It's common in both men and women who achieve success. There are several lies at work behind imposter syndrome. "I'm not good enough," and "there's something wrong with me" are the usual culprits.

But for women, there's often an additional factor at play behind imposter syndrome—the feeling that they're failing to act with integrity.

Having integrity essentially means being authentic, and taking actions that are in alignment with your moral and ethical values. It sounds pretty straightforward, but it isn't always easy to act on. First of all, acting with integrity often takes courage. Second, sometimes it's hard to know which part of yourself to express authentically.

Think back to the chapter when we discussed the difference between men's and women's brains. Women's brains are typically more "balanced" than men's. We use both sides of our brains for a task that men use one side for. This not only means we're more attuned to our environments; it means we're more capable of juggling logic and emotion, reason and intuition.

If we want to speak with integrity, we want to express everything we know to be true—both the logical and the intuitive aspects.

However, we also tailor our communication styles based on who we're speaking to. For example, if you're the only woman in a conference full of men talking about where to take the company, it's unlikely you're going to feel comfortable talking about your intuition. You'll probably be more inclined to stick with logical lines of discussion, so your points will be taken seriously.

On the other hand, if you're sitting in a feminine leadership circle, the women present are going to be more receptive to your intuition, your energy, and what you feel. They'll be more likely to dismiss logical trains of thought, since they're operating from the premise that energy is what aligns and organizes the world.

The logical folks don't want to talk about energy, and the feeling folks don't want to talk logic. What's a brain-balanced energy-aware businesswoman to do?

One client of mine came from a background as an electrical engineer. She was starting a coaching business, and approaching

"energy" from a whole different angle. She knew about energy as electricity, shooting through wires and engineered structures, but she also knew that energy infuses our thoughts and emotions, and by shifting our energy around a situation, we shift our experience of that situation.

As a coach, she had plenty of credentials and experience, but she still felt like a fake. It was especially a problem when she was interviewed by men, who didn't connect with her understanding of energy as a force they could align themselves and their companies with, to generate the results they desired.

She had to approach these conversations from a purely logical place, and this felt inauthentic to her. She felt as though she had abandoned her integrity, and she felt like an imposter.

The same dynamic comes into play in a variety of situations. Logically, you could fit another appointment into your schedule, but emotionally you know it would be the wrong decision. Logically, you know that a career in the arts isn't statistically likely to provide abundant income, but intuitively and emotionally, you know it's the right path for you. You know there's limited science to back up alternative medicine, but you practice it and experience healing anyway.

In situations like these, our intuition is invaluable. It tells us what kind of conversation we're having—a logical one, or a more energy-based one. It tells us whether our new friend will be open to hearing we used homeopathy and herbs to heal ourselves, or whether she'll say, "That's a load of hogwash!" It tells us not to talk about energy alignment in an interview for a corporate desk job.

If we can be aware of all aspects of our truth, we can consciously choose how to present ourselves in order to connect with others. This isn't being inauthentic, and it's not stepping outside our integrity. It's using our heightened awareness to make our way through the world.

Women do this all the time. It comes very naturally to most of us. We put on business suits when going to meetings, and sexy dresses when going on dates. We use different tones of voice and words when talking to babies and children than with other adults. We change our clothes, our hair, our makeup, our shoes, and our mannerisms depending on the company we're in and the situation.

For those times when you're really not sure which way to go, or you can't shake imposter syndrome, get in touch with your intuition. There are a few exercises below that will help with that.

Fortunately, it's becoming more acceptable to have conversations about feminine principles and intuition in the business world—especially in women-owned businesses. As women step into their power, and the masculine-driven arena sees our success, it's going to become clear that we use some different methods. It's going to become more common to discuss different methods of running business, life, and the world.

Exercises:
Can you think of a time when you tailored your conversation so the other party could relate to you? What did you know that you didn't share? Why did you decide to only share specific things? Do you think you made the right decision?

A powerful way to get in touch with your intuition is to listen to your body. Consider a decision you've been struggling to make. First, write about your dilemma below. What makes this such a difficult decision?

Next, sit quietly and think about the problem. What sensations do you notice in your body? Is there a tightness in your belly? A recoiling in your heart? A heaviness in your head?

Focus on this sensation. Ask it what it's trying to tell you, and then listen. Write your first impressions of this message here.

Oftentimes, that provides the guidance you need. If you'd like a little more clarity, take some time to imagine each possible outcome of the decision before you, and let your body tell you how it feels in each scenario. What were some of the best physical sensations you had during this exercise? What imagined outcomes were they connected to?

Chapter Seventeen

Characteristics of Feminine Leadership

"Strength to lead has to do with being trusted, and trust has to do with having qualities and experience needed for whatever the particular task is."
— Dr. Jean Shinoda Bolen

In the last chapter, I promised I'd discuss a few ways feminine leadership manifests in practice. Here you have it! This is a beautiful list of heart-felt practices that can change your experience of business and life overall.

Feminine Leadership is balanced. When we lead from our hearts and intuition, and combine that with powerful and effective action, magic happens. These qualities emerge naturally. However, we can also learn to develop our hearts and intuition from practicing these characteristics.

Some of the characteristics are skills we need to develop, like fostering healthy relationships and working with energy. And these methods take as much practice and dedication as the skills needed to run business from a masculine mindset. Using your intuition to forecast the future of the market takes as much skill as forecasting the future of the market by analyzing present and past trends. It's just a different kind of skill.

Connection

Women lead through connection and collaboration with others. Research shows that women tend to be more social in business, whereas men treat it more like a hierarchy. We value real relationships with our clients, and we value the input and contributions of our team. We aren't interested in an environment where every team member simply fills an empty space, like cogs in a machine. Instead, success is determined by collaborative effort, and even collaborative vision.

Women are also skilled at empathizing, connecting with others, and making people feel comfortable. This is one reason many companies—even those primarily staffed by men—often have female HR departments.

Relationships

Good relationships are the bedrock of every successful venture the world has ever seen—in business and otherwise. Being more social than men, we women are natural relationship builders. We're able to create close-knit communities that stand together emotionally as well as professionally.

In today's world, social media is replacing traditional "push" marketing methods. Traditional marketing is designed like a hierarchy, disseminating a carefully crafted bit of information in a carefully chosen way to a specifically researched demographic. It wasn't important for a company to have a direct relationship with its customers. But as social media gains more power, that relationship is becoming very relevant. And people's relationships with each other are more powerful than ever.

Intuition

If the market tells a woman to take her company down a bright and sunny road, but she feels better about the dark and shady path that barely anyone's taking—she'll follow her gut.

It's not that women ignore statistics, research, and projections. It's that, after taking in the relevant information, we still make decisions based on what feels right for ourselves, our company and our team. And if we don't trust someone, we won't work with them.

Inter-Connection

We understand that being connected with others is important. But we also understand that everything is connected. It's impossible to make an "isolated" decision that only affects one aspect of our business, or one of our team members. Each part affects the whole.

This is true for the microcosm and the macrocosm. A feminine leader isn't interested in success if it comes at the expense of something, such as a group of people or the environment. A single decision has ripples that affect the entire organization, society, and even the world. We are part of something bigger than ourselves.

That's why the bottom line isn't a woman's main objective. There is no "bottom line." It's all up, or it's all down.

Making Our Own Luck

The saying goes that opportunity doesn't knock twice. We're supposed to jump at Lady Luck when she shows up, because she doesn't stay around for long.

Well, we understand that opportunity doesn't knock twice—it knocks again and again until we answer the door! By continually showing up and doing our best work, by committing to success, we place ourselves in the path of luck. This means great opportunities are always falling in our laps!

We don't have to take opportunities that arise at the wrong time, or that involve the wrong people. We invite Lady Luck to lunch instead of hoping she comes around knocking.

Energy

Everything that shows up in our lives is a manifestation of the energy behind it. Women living their brilliance understand this on an intuitive level. While the masculine is busy trying to manipulate matter, the feminine quietly attunes herself to the energy behind the matter, and consciously shifts it to create what she wants in the world.

Understanding the nature of energy, we take the time to sense the energy of our team and our current situation, and assess whether that energy is in alignment with our intentions. If not, we can shift the energy, like turning the dial on a radio to a different frequency.

Being attuned to energy contributes to our ability to sense how a person is feeling—our empathy and intuition—which means we're better able to connect with and understand others, create harmony, and make positive decisions.

Being in the Flow

Being in the flow means we're attuned to the energy of our intentions, and we're acting from our intuition. That may seem like a lot to manage, but when it's happening, it comes quite naturally. When we're in the flow, we find our work simple, and things magically come together to support our success. This is when we experience coincidence and synchronicity.

So if all this is true, then where has this information been all our lives? Why didn't our mothers teach us this stuff? Because they were trying to train us out of it! In a masculine-dominated culture, our feminine traits aren't respected; they are scorned and oppressed. Our mothers were afraid that we wouldn't get what we needed in life if we relied on our feminine advantages.

Chapter Eighteen

The Future of Women-Owned Businesses

"I believe that the thought that women together can change the world is emerging into the minds and hearts of many of us, and that the vessel for personal and planetary evolution is the circle with a spiritual center."
— Dr. Jean Shinoda Bolen

How powerful are the lessons our mothers taught us—the lessons ingrained in our psyches by society? Very.

While feminine influence is rising in the world, including in business, women still have a long way to go before we're on equal standing with men.

As of 2012, only 3.6% of Fortune 500 companies were owned by women. That's 18 companies out of 500. And 2012 was a record high, up from 12 companies in 2011. In all, only one out of every 10 companies on the Fortune 500 list had women on their boards.

While we probably won't see anything close to a 50/50 split between men and women CEOs in the next few decades, it's encouraging that there are so many women in the pipeline ready to step into leadership positions. Many women sit just below the top level chairs in Fortune 500 companies, and as soon as there's movement and turnaround in the company, they're poised to assume leadership.

Even so, we probably won't see a huge shift in the way these companies are run. A single female CEO doesn't mean a company is run with feminine leadership values. More than likely, a woman in such a position will continue running the company as it's been run in the past, with a few changes here and there, but nothing that will be too controversial or cause her male colleagues to look sideways at her.

The biggest momentum is happening in the small business sector. In 2013, the U.S. Small Business Administration reported that women-owned businesses were the fastest growing sector in the country, with over 200,000 new businesses in the previous year alone being owned and run by women.

While those numbers are encouraging, most women-owned businesses fail to scale and produce as much profit as their maleowned counterparts.

There are any number of reasons for this. Historically, women in business have had less access to loans and capital than men. That's changed a little under the Obama administration, with the Small Business Association three to five times more likely to award loans to women. Even so, women tend to be more fiscally conservative when running businesses, and less likely to go into debt to start up or stay afloat.

Also, women tend to put the needs of their employees over the desire for rapid growth.

Right now, the world is experiencing an economic crisis. In general, industries that were rapidly booming are now slowing down. With this in mind, it's possible that businesses that don't experience rapid growth, but find a place of stability and establish themselves, are more likely to be successful in the long run.

We can say it's unfortunate that women-owned businesses don't grow at the rate of male-owned ones, but we can also say that thanks to their "slow and steady" mindset and tendency to avoid too much debt, they stand a good chance of survival in a poor economic climate.

Speaking of the economic crisis, it was masculine ways of thinking and working that got us here. We can't solve a problem using the same principles it was created with. The world needs the feminine approach to leadership to guide us out of this mess, into a more sustainable, pleasurable world that generates long-term profits.

The world is waking up to the value and power of the feminine, and we're realizing that what we've feared and disrespected is actually the key to our success—as women, and as the human race. The more we honor what we are, the more success we have. And the more success we have, the more respect the world (and the masculine) gives us … and the more the feminine is raised up from where she's been held down.

Part Six

The Eight Truths of Feminine Freedom

Earlier, we learned about the seven lies that have held us back from our full feminine brilliance. Throughout the book, we've discussed the power that feminine traits have to help us create lives and businesses that resonate with our deepest truths, our most passionate purposes, and our wild souls. We've discussed what those feminine traits are, how they evolved differently from masculine traits, and how they manifest in an organization. We've also discussed different blocks we might have to accessing our feminine brilliance.

Now, we're going to focus on how to access it.

We can do this by focusing on eight ways to live that help us reverse the seven lies.

When we live these truths, we live from a place of authenticity and courage. Instead of making decisions based on what other people want—or our finances, or our fears—we're listening to and honoring our hearts, staying aligned with our values and our vision. If we adopt these principles as our way of life, we find ourselves living by our own code—one that empowers us instead of oppresses us.

Another key to feminine brilliance is being part of a community of like-minded, like-hearted women, and it's especially powerful if this group gathers together in a circle. There's something about circles that allows women to come together in a truly supportive, collaborative way; the face-to-face meeting allows us to ground our wisdom, intuition, and experiences. Circles enable us to guide and encourage one another as we develop our brilliance, and lean into our true callings. Once women get involved in circles like this, they often realize they've been craving this kind of connection their whole lives. It's as though a sacred bond of sisterhood is finally fulfilled.

It's one thing to believe in the power of feminine leadership, but another thing to be able to utilize it in a way that transforms the way you relate to, and experience, life. Are you ready?

Chapter Nineteen

Truth 1: Open Your Circuits

"You are not merely the physical body that you identify with out of habit. Your essential state is a field of infinite possibilities."
— Deepak Chopra

Imagine you're a light bulb, and you're surrounded by hundreds of batteries on every side. The batteries represent different aspects of your life and your being. One is for your intuition; another is for your community, another for your body, and so on. You have hundreds of potential power sources to ignite your spark and turn on your light.

But you're not connected to the batteries, so your light doesn't shine. You might not even know there are any batteries out there.

We need to open our circuits, recognize these power sources, and connect to them. What does that look like in the real world? It means becoming aware that we have resources—intuition, a wise body, a circle of women, a community of friends and partners willing to help us, etc.—and then being willing to connect with those power sources in a meaningful way.

We are surrounded every day by literally hundreds of untapped resources. Some of these are as close as our bodies and breath—the practice of deep breathing is a resource, as is yoga, exercise, clean eating, and the wisdom that lives in your body. (We'll detail how to access this wisdom in a few chapters, but taking care of your body is a big part of it.) Some of these resources are more external—such as classes, colleagues, or technology that helps you complete a project.

It's a good idea to open your "inner circuits" (get in touch with your own body wisdom) at the same time as focusing on the "external circuits." The more connected you are with yourself and your own wisdom, the more opportunity will come your way. Not only will you notice more opportunity, but it will literally be attracted to you as you get in the flow and get connected.

Open your circuits, notice more resources, attract more opportunities, notice more opportunities … can you see how this effect starts to spiral?

When we're not living in our brilliance, when we're domesticated or running on autopilot, we often feel shut down, closed off, and alone—as though we have no options. But in fact, our options are around every corner. When you open your circuits, you literally can't blink without experiencing possibility all around you.

Don't just acknowledge that your body has wisdom. Spend time with your body sensations and connect with them. What are they trying to tell you? How could you best honor them?

Don't just nod your head and agree that you could connect with hundreds of potential clients on social media. Reach out!

Don't just say you believe that people in your life would be willing to help you out if you asked for a favor. The next time someone says, "Let me know if there's anything I can do to help," don't be afraid to say, "You know what? There is." People —especially women—love to be needed.

Exercises:
Take a piece of paper … and better make it a big one, or be sure you have several sheets. Now, write every resource you can think of that you have in your life. This includes friends, family, tools like computers and libraries, transportation, software programs, self-help books, etc. Anything or anyone that could potentially provide any sort of support for you whatsoever. Write it all out. This is your Source Sheet.

Now, sit back and consider a problem that's been on your mind lately. Look at your Source Sheet. It's likely that almost every source on your sheet could help you with this problem in some way, but it's also likely that some sources are more appropriate for the issue at hand. Put a star by at least 20 relevant sources. In what ways have you utilized them? In what ways have you overlooked their potential? Brainstorm different ways to use these sources to solve the problem on your mind.

Chapter Twenty

Truth 2: Stay Wild

"When you recover or discover something that nourishes your soul and brings joy, care enough about yourself to make room for it in your life."
— Dr. Jean Shinoda Bolen

Staying wild means finding your brilliance and honoring it, even if it's inconvenient (and it often feels that way at first).

Bring your passions out to play. Do something that moves you, and do it every day. And if you're not sure what moves you, seek your wisdom through your deep wound. Do something that makes your heart sing and ache at the same time.

For example, a friend of mine wasn't sure where her brilliance lay—what moved her and helped her move the world. She got in touch with her body, meditated and journaled daily, but still didn't feel as though she had direction that would allow her to live with purpose, express her wildness, or find her freedom.

We were having coffee one day, just talking, and she saw a poster on the coffee shop community board for a lost dog. She immediately began talking with deep passion about how neglected animals need safe havens and loving caretakers. I could tell this was a powerful subject for her, and she said it stemmed from her childhood, when one of her favorite dogs had died. The experience had affected her deeply, leaving her feeling helpless as her beloved pet suffered, and even all these years later, she nearly teared up while talking about it.

I was struck with inspiration. I suggested that maybe she'd been seeking her wildness in ways that other women would have defined it. But all the while, she had this passionate heart, and had been writing off its desire to care for animals as a lost cause—she still felt helpless. She hadn't considered her own passions important or valid enough to guide her brilliance.

She wound up working at an animal shelter and leading fundraisers for non-profits to help abused, neglected, and homeless animals. It meant a pay cut for her, since she left a corporate job, but it also meant living in alignment with her heart's values and feeling like she was making a real difference in the world.

That's what I mean by do something that makes your heart sing and ache at the same time. It's interesting—our brilliance really does light up our lives. Without it, we're in the dark. We aren't sure where to go or what to do. With it, we suddenly have a lamp on a dark path.

Another way to get in touch with your wildness, is to make self-care and growth a priority. Self-care means more than taking a hot bath at the end of the day, although that can certainly be a powerful restorative. Self-care means finding those things that melt your stress away—leave you feeling balanced and happy—and working them into every day. Maybe it's writing in your journal or practicing yoga. Maybe it's singing karaoke, or having time to yourself every day.

Whatever your self-care entails, make sure to make time for it. Write it into your schedule, and guard that time. It may mean pushing deadlines back, or taking on fewer commitments. It may mean reassessing your priorities—getting clear about what your priorities really are (is your priority really going to the school play, or is it being a good mother?), and getting creative about finding ways to meet them.

Your self-care will be vital as you tap into your brilliance and allow it to take center stage in your life. Your brilliant talents have always wanted center stage. Your queen has always wanted her throne. But pleasing others, believing you're not good enough, hurrying up, and other lies have taken the spotlight and the crown. Time to take your place once more!

You may have to eliminate some negatives from your life. If there are commitments, jobs, projects or people that just leave you feeling drained, contribute nothing to your life, and make you groan with grief anytime you have to deal with them … cut them loose, if at all possible.

One way to get at the heart of your priorities is to ask yourself what would happen if you failed to do a certain task. Would you feel relieved (a sign to deprioritize the task), would you feel disappointed (a sign that this task is an important priority for you), or would you feel uncomfortable (a sign that the task is a priority, but one you're not too thrilled about).

When you prioritize, you're not being cruel or selfish. You're taking responsibility for your time, and making room for your brilliance. The world has been cruel, authoritative, and oppressive of your brilliance. You're allowed to be stern and create some boundaries. You're allowed to make your own rules. Trust me—you'll be an inspiration to yourself and to others!

Be gentle with yourself. If you loop back into those seven old lies and find yourself putting your needs on the back burner while you take care of someone else's, don't beat yourself up. Simply, and gently, switch the position of the pots. (Notice we're not taking anything off the stove here! We're just shifting priorities.)

Chapter Twenty-One

Truth 3: Get Embodied

"If there is a single definition of healing, it is to enter with mercy and awareness those pains, mental and physical, from which we have withdrawn in judgment and dismay."
— Dr. Stephen Levine

Masculine society doesn't acknowledge the wisdom of the body. This isn't surprising—body wisdom isn't derived from logic or intellect. It's difficult to quantify, measure, and turn into predictable formulas:

$A + B = C$

Tension around your heart + an uncomfortable conversation with a client = taking the company in a different direction … sometimes!

The elements in the second equation could lead to a different solution every time! And without clearly defined guidelines that produce predictable outcomes, men often just don't know what to do or how to react to the fluid experiences of life. Wanting structured systems and predictable solutions is natural to them. This is how they feel most secure, and capable of protecting their clans.

But our bodies are deeply, essentially wise. Our bodies carry information about what we need more of, or less of. They carry resonant energy from experiences of our past, and can cause us to repeat those experiences whether we want to or not. Our bodies react positively to people who bring out the best in us, while instinctively withdrawing from people who could pose a threat, either physically, mentally, or emotionally.

This is just the tip of the iceberg! Our bodies contain maps that can help us navigate all the unpredictable ups and downs of life.

Learn to read these maps. Become more aware of the sensations in your body. Commit to spending time with them, and to understanding what those sensations are trying to tell you.

Think you don't know how to listen to your body? Quick—do you have to go to the bathroom? Do you have a headache? Are you hungry, or full? Are you craving anything? Does your elbow hurt from that old injury?

Easy answers, right?

See? You already have the tools you need to get embodied. You were born with them. We're going to call these body signals "felt sense," because it's not thought, it's not emotion, and it's not desire. It's more primal than all that.

Most of us only scratch the surface of our felt sense. For instance, we know when we're in pain, when we're hungry, or when we have to go to the bathroom. But felt sense goes much deeper than this. Here are some possible ways felt sense can give you direction:

You drank a little too much water; you really need to pee. Go to the bathroom.

Your shoes are too tight; your feet hurt. Take them off and wiggle your toes.

This light is too bright; you're squinting. Put on some sunglasses.

This person isn't listening to you; your heart feels tight and closed off. End the conversation.

Your job isn't aligned with your purpose; you feel like your limbs are tight or restrained, and you want to cry. Time to look for a new position.

Your felt sense responds to people, environments, fears, desires, trauma, joy, and virtually every situation you can think of.

We've been taught to ignore those sensations, and to forge ahead regardless of what our bodies are feeling or trying to tell us. We've been raised as "walking heads," disconnected from our bodies.

If we're accustomed to living in a way that makes our bodies uncomfortable, or if we're walking around with the memory of trauma in our tissues, it's no wonder we're disconnected from our body wisdom! It's much easier to ignore what's uncomfortable, rather than take the time to feel it and make the shifts to change discomfort to pleasure.

When you're living your brilliance, your body will tell you. It will wake up, and you'll find yourself full of energy and vitality. Spots of tension will ease and you'll feel more pleasure than in the past. Your body will become a sacred partner, rather than a tool you barely take note of.

Exercise:
For women, the womb and lower abdomen is the source of power, centeredness, and mental and emotional clarity. It's what connects us to our intuition, body sense, and joy. So many women have lost touch with how it feels to be deeply centered in the womb. This exercise is one that you'll want to practice at least daily, and perhaps multiple times a day. It will connect you to the abundant and rich flow of grounded spiritual energy. Women thrive on this connection, and the inner glow that it creates. And because feeling good in your body—pleasure—always creates clarity in decision-making, this exercise also leads to more profitable businesses, and that always leads to a happier and more fulfilled life. Real power is not about control or domination, but about flexibility and clarity.

Sit in a comfortable position with your back straight. Take a deep breath, and let go of all the chatter and noise the world wants to bring to your doorstep. Have you noticed that when you take a deep breath and fully release it, your mind begins to slow down? Take few deep breaths, long and slow, and feel yourself relax.

Focus on the area in your lower belly, and imagine a channel of light running between your heart and your womb. Now notice your lower abdomen. Feel the energy moving there, as you begin to notice your seat in the chair that you're sitting on, and your feet on the floor.

Notice that as you think about this, you can feel a growing energy in your womb. It might even feel like a ring of energy around your hips, like a hula-hoop. Now imagine that running down the center of your body is a channel connecting your head, heart and womb, and extending into the earth. Notice the energy from the earth coming up to meet your body, and flowing up through this channel.

As you breathe in, imagine energy coming up through your body, and as you breathe out, it flows back to the earth. You may notice it feels like you're breathing in and out through the womb and lower body. This is a place that you can always come back to when you're tired, stressed, worried, or feeling unsure. It's your body-centered home.

Chapter Twenty-Two

Truth 4: Listen to Your Intuition

"I firmly believe that intuitive or symbolic sight is not a gift but a skill—a skill based in self-esteem."
— Caroline Myss

Intuition goes hand in hand with body wisdom. Like body wisdom, intuition is discredited by masculine culture as being groundless, illogical, and "woo-woo." The art of making decisions based on intuition isn't widely acknowledged or respected.

But intuition is wiser than logic. Intuition recognizes that energy is behind everything we see (and want to see), and it can find routes to success that logic is blind to. Intuition is based on the big picture. Logic is based on pieces of information. Intuition takes emotion into account. Logic ignores it.

Our intuition shows up in a variety of ways. Sometimes we experience it as a physical sensation (another reason it's so important to be embodied), and sometimes we have a deep knowing. It can show up as a gut feeling, a hunch, a strong emotion that won't be ignored, or a dream we have at night. It can also show up in external ways, such as signs or omens in the world. Sometimes intuition looks like coincidence or synchronicity.

A big key to accessing your intuition is feeling your body and noticing what is happening. If you can feel your body's sensations, reactions, and deeply held energies, you can discern what your body is telling you. But as I've said, intuition speaks to you in more ways than one.

When you're being guided in a certain direction, your body will know. However, the energy field around you will also organize itself toward giving you that direction. Your emotions will respond. External events may begin to take on symbolism. For example, you come down with a sore throat when you need to express yourself more clearly. Or your car breaks down when you've hit a dead-end in your career—you literally aren't going anywhere!

Little synchronicities may occur that catch your attention. You may wonder what you can do to feel more centered, and the next day you come across an article about meditation, one of your friends mentions meditation in a conversation, and someone references it in a radio interview you catch in the car. Pretty clear the universe is answering your question!

Why does this work? Because the external world is a reflection of your internal state.

Once you think the universe has answered, take some time to hold that answer in your body and see how it feels. This will reassure you that you've received the right communication.

Look out for number repetitions, like catching the clock at 1:11 several times over several days. These are little winks and nudges from your guides and the energy field around you, as they try to get your attention.

So the main trick to intuition is being aware and listening. Listen to your body, to your emotions, to the world around you.

This is how we separate intuition from anxiety and fear, expectation and desire.

Chapter Twenty-Three

Truth 5: Move Through Fear

"Tell your heart that the fear of suffering is worse than the suffering itself. And that no heart has ever suffered when it goes in search of its dreams, because every second of the search is a second's encounter with God and with eternity."
— Paulo Coelho

It's natural to feel afraid when we're venturing into uncharted territory, trying something new, or standing up for our freedom in ways we never have before. Fear of others' reactions, financial repercussions, and an uncertain future can tempt us to backtrack into safer territory.

I'm going to boil all these fears down into one single drive, which is really at the root of all fear:

The fear of loss.

When we're afraid of other's reactions, we're afraid of losing their approval. When we're afraid of financial repercussions, we're afraid of losing money or possessions we've worked hard for. When we're afraid of an uncertain outcome, we're afraid of losing the sense of security we have, even if its uncomfortable.

This process starts when we're very young—some say it starts right out of the womb, after we lose that constant warmth, nourishment, and security. From an early age, we learn that what we love and take pleasure from can go away. At some point, our lives become less about enjoying what's happening now, and more about avoiding loss.

In the areas of your life that aren't working, how much avoidance and fear of loss is at work? How many of these selfprotective games have you played?

Quit before you start. If you don't enter the game (that's any aspect of life you're avoiding), you can't lose.

Quit in mid-stream. If you quit before the game is over, you might be a quitter, but you've saved yourself from being a "loser."

"That's OK, I didn't care anyway." You never committed to it anyway, so it doesn't matter that you lost.

Dumb game. If you decide the game's stupid, it doesn't matter that you lost.

Endless game. If you keep halfheartedly playing the game without ever coming to a place where you win or lose, then at least you haven't lost.

It's okay if you recognized yourself in any of those examples—or even all of them. You don't have to be perfect, and you don't have to eradicate fear and discomfort. The important thing is to recognize that you're letting fear of loss block your brilliance.

We have to understand the difference between discomfort that means we're growing, and discomfort that means we're doing the wrong thing. Our intuition and our bodies can help with this.

But the most powerful force we can harness to counteract fear is love. In his excellent book, *What Happy People Know*, Dr. Dan Baker talks about fear and love:

"We need to be willing to charge headlong into the inferno of our most horrific fears – eyes open, intellect and spirit at the ready.... That takes courage, and that's when courage is one of the prerequisites for happiness. But where does that ability come from? What power grants the strength to overcome the sick, shaky feeling of fear? Only one power is that strong: love. In the ultimate analysis, human beings have only two essential, primal feelings: fear and love.

Fear compels us to survive, and love enables us to thrive.… For you to be happy, love must lead this dance."

Love can help you shift your habits and attitude to a more courageous, creative setting.

How can we practice love in the face of fear and uncertainty? Again, we can get in touch with our bodies. Find where the fear lives within you, visualize it as its own conscious entity, and have a conversation with it. Ask it what it's afraid of. Then ask if that's really what it's afraid of, or if there's a deeper fear behind the first. Ask your fear if it's trying to hurt you, or hold you back, or if it's only trying to protect you. Feel that—the force of how powerfully this fear wants to keep you safe and sound. Feel how the real motivation, even behind fear, is deep, sincere (if misguided) love. Thank your fear for being there for you; for protecting you all this time. And then make it a deal. It won't want to go anywhere if it's not sure you'll be okay. So ask if it will step aside for a time, and let you move ahead toward your goals. Tell it that it's allowed to come back and protect you again if things don't go well. Tell it you're not angry with it; you're grateful.

If we can learn to appreciate even the seemingly negative forces that surround us, we can practice love in the darkness.

If you're stepping into your brilliance and you don't feel brave, that's okay. Do it afraid. You don't have to eliminate all fear, and you don't have to embody perfect love. You only have to face the fear, and move gently through it. Don't let fear lead you to decisions that aren't right for you.

"Remembering that you are going to die is the best way I know to avoid the trap of thinking you have something to lose. You are already naked. There is no reason not to follow your heart."
— Steve Jobs

Exercises:
Make a list of a few places in your life or business that make you feel uncertain, or even skeptical that things could work out. Then make a list of reasons why it might work or have a positive outcome.

I'm not so sure about:

It will be okay because:

Chapter Twenty-Four

Truth 6: Find Your Sisterhood

PATHWAYS: "Why does God incarnate?"
KW: "It's no fun having dinner alone."
— From an interview with Ken Wilbur done by Pathways

Every wild woman needs a sisterhood. You might call this your tribe. It's important to find like-minded women and connect with them on a regular basis. Having a strong network of people who think like you and understand your brilliance can be vital to staying courageous, moving through fear, believing in yourself, and making decisions based on passion.

Finding your sisterhood requires conscious decision making regarding who you spend your time with. As you go about daily life, you typically encounter the same people, such as co-workers, classmates, or moms who have kids the same age as yours. Sometimes, you'll find soul connections among these people. Other times, the friendships developed here are more shallow and short-term, based around the circumstances rather than on any real bond of sisterhood.

There's nothing wrong with this. However, remember that the people around you have a big impact on you—especially on how you spend your time, what you believe is possible, and how much you grow.

For example, if you want to start your own business, you're going to need encouragement and connection with other women in your position, and women who have achieved what you want to achieve. You'll find this invaluable on your journey. The people around you from day to day may not be interested in what you're doing, or think you're aiming too high, or they may not understand where you're coming from in conversations. They may not have experienced advice to offer, and they even may be turned off by your new direction in life and what they see as your new values.

All this can really put a damper on your plans for a new business.

No one grows alone. Growth always involves support in one way or another. The exchange of ideas and encouragement that takes place in a true sisterhood can make all the difference in your business and your life.

Finding a tribe of women who are aligned with your energy doesn't always happen without effort. But you may be surprised at how easily things fall into place with just a little work on your part. Here are a few ideas:

- Align with a group of successful women in business
- Take a class for women entrepreneurs.
- Look for group classes or meetings around your brilliance—if you enjoy singing, look for a choir. If you enjoy cooking, look for a cooking class.

Look for group classes or meetings around your brilliance—if you enjoy singing, look for a choir. If you enjoy cooking, look for a cooking class.

Another idea is to start your own women's circle. Archeological evidence proves that women have been sitting in circles for literally thousands of years. Sitting in a circle creates a psychological shift—instead of looking to one person at the front of the group, who is expected to give some kind of presentation or guidance, everyone in the circle sees themselves as equal, and capable of contributing to the group. Instead of a lecture, a discussion ensues, and everyone is able to learn and teach together.

This can lighten some of the pressure on the group's leader, so she doesn't feel forced to have a presentation prepared.

Your sisterhood can help you get connected, so even as you honor your individual strengths and practice your brilliance, you never have to feel alone. You're never without a strong network of support to get you through the rough times, help you stay your course, and provide clarity and insight when you need it most.

We need collaborative feminine circles. Our society is changing faster than ever, and we face enormous challenges that can only be addressed with a different mindset, different values, and different actions than we've used in the past. When empowered women connect, they develop a deep collective power for change and support.

I like the visual of a red scarf based on the story told about Isadora Duncan. After dancing Tchaikovsky's *Marche Slave* in Boston, Isadora Duncan grabbed the red scarves attached to her costume and lifted them up, shouting, "This is RED and so I am I—it is the color of life and vigor! You were once wild here, don't let them tame you!" As the scarves were lifted, she revealed her bare breasts to the audience, prompting the mayor of Boston to ban any further performances from her.

Circles are opportunities for women to engage in conversations that matter, and to experience what it feels like to be part of a collaboration, where every chair holds a woman who feels powerful, profitable and like a leader.

The face-to-face connection is important, but living the experience of the feminine is life changing. It's only with the body experience that women really "get it." Women gather in small groups to remember and to relearn to live the eight truths, let go of the seven lies, get in touch with our bodies, tap into our intuition, and empower one another to live our brilliance.

"As we look ahead into the next century, leaders will be those who empower others."
— Bill Gates

It's also a good idea to find a coach or mentor to work with—someone passionate about helping women express their brilliance and take their lives to the next level. When choosing a mentor, it's important to be clear with yourself what you're looking to accomplish. Some coaches focus on helping women develop strong businesses, others focus on relationships, and others focus on helping women become coaches. Some coaches focus on life overall. So first, understand what you hope to accomplish or where you need guidance, then seek a mentor with a proven track record of helping women just like you.

Chapter Twenty-Five

Truth 7: Lead Brilliantly

"You are not a passive observer in the cosmos. The entire universe is expressing itself through you at this very moment."
— Jean Houston

Leading brilliantly means you're living your purpose with no apologies. You're utilizing the practices of feminine leadership, valuing your relationships and making your own luck. And you're not afraid to express all your most feminine qualities—such as your patience, vulnerability, integrity and kindness.

It's your divine feminine right to live with such passion and purpose.

No matter what your religion, spirituality or scientific beliefs are, you're blessed to be here. You're the result of millions of years of evolution designed to create the strongest, wisest, most attractive and best-prepared person there is.

Do you think that was an accident?

You're capable of the very best things imaginable in life. But that's not always easy to recognize. When you live brilliantly, your attitude naturally reflects your positive experience. You become a more positive person, and positive people are attractive in many ways. Your attitude can transform you from a magnet for failure to a magnate of success.

By acknowledging your own greatness, other people will acknowledge it in you. The more they recognize drive and confidence in other people, the more they'll see it in themselves—and look up to you for showing it to them!

The bottom line is, it is all-important and beyond sensible to recognize that you are great and that you are capable of great things. Take a moment to think about the people that you admire: the artists of varying kinds, athletes, public figures or even members of your own family. Do you think that they achieved what they did, and helped people to feel as good about themselves and of life as they did, by playing small and being afraid?

You may be surprised at the reactions you get when you step into your brilliance. Before you even realize it, other women will be looking at you as an inspiration and telling themselves, "If she can do it, maybe I can do it, too." Maybe you've said that yourself about a strong woman in your own life.

Chapter Twenty-Six

Truth 8: Focus on What Matters

"Just as you would not neglect seeds that you planted with hope that they will bear vegetables and fruits and flowers, so you must attend to nourish the garden of your becoming."
— Jean Houston

Focusing on what matters all comes back to listening to your heart. When we listen to our hearts, it's much easier to prioritize in a way that cultivates pleasure and success. Part of the work of becoming wild, wise and free is clearing the clutter away from our hearts, sounding out the truth, and developing the courage to honor it.

In chapter five, we talked about all the various roles you play as a woman—an employee, an employer, a wife or partner, a mother, a daughter, a caretaker, and so on. It's easy to let any one of these roles overwhelm the others, and take over most of your time and mental space. In other words, it's easy to lose sight of what really matters, and before you know it, you're not leading your life—your life is leading you.

To reclaim your life and lead brilliantly, you need to make the main thing the main thing. Here are a few questions that can help. Answering these can guide you to the heart of … well, of your own heart!

If your doctor told you that you could only work two hours a day, what would you do with that time?

If your doctor told you that you could only work two hours a week, what would you do?

What would you spend the rest of your time doing?

Why would you spend the most time doing these things? Why do they matter?

Make a habit of looking at yourself in the mirror each morning, and asking one of Steve Jobs's favorite questions: If today were the last day of my life, would I be happy doing what I'm about to do? It's okay if the answer is no once, twice, or a few times. But if you find yourself consistently saying no, it's time to make a change.

What are the top three activities you engage in that are really time-consumers, but make you feel as though you've been productive?

You'll notice these questions aren't so much about time management. Instead, they're about focus. If all you're doing is parceling out your time between unimportant tasks, you won't get much of value done even if you become a master of time management. However, if you learn the art of managing your own attention, and giving it to those things that have the most impact on your ilfe, you'll develop a habit for happiness.

"Deciding what not to do is as important as deciding what to do."
— Steve Jobs

Don't hesitate to use your embodiment practice and intuition to determine your right path, too. Your body and your intuition often have a clearer vision for your future than your mind. So get primal. Get wild. And get free.

Part Seven

The Real Power of Positive Thinking

Chapter Twenty-Seven

What is Positivity?

"You have the power to heal your life, and you need to know that. We think so often that we are helpless, but we're not. We always have the power of our mind. Claim and consciously use your power."
— Louise L. Hay

If awareness is the foundation for creating a life of freedom and brilliance, positive thinking is the cornerstone. Without awareness, we won't understand where and how we want to grow, and without positive thinking, we won't believe it's possible, or that we deserve it. Positivity is essential for designing a life full of joy, inner peace, and brilliance.

Before we go any further, let's talk about positivity itself. Basically, positivity means having an optimistic mindset. Even when times are hard, our thoughts are reassuring and hopeful, and we can find the silver lining in any situation. This may sound like Pollyanna thinking, but it is so much more. Positivity doesn't mean you never have a negative thought. It's not about denying the darkness; it's about focusing on the light, however dim it may seem, and knowing you have the power to make it brighter.

It's also not about suppressing negative emotions. As we've discussed in several places throughout the book, suppressing traumatic experiences, and the negative emotions they inspire, is often a knee-jerk reaction—the "freeze" response in "fight, flight or freeze." This energy isn't released. Instead, it's stored in our bodies; it resurfaces in subsequent instances of stress, and expresses itself over the years as chronic pain and illness.

That's not a positive experience at all!

So if we're going to live positively, we need to discharge the negative energy that collects in our bodies—both from past experiences, and from new sources of tension we encounter from day to day. A practice of embodiment is so powerful here.

Being positive is a choice, and a mindset we can actively cultivate. As human beings, our fundamental dignity lies in our ability to choose, and to be the conscious cause of the effects we experience. Positivity encourages a sense of self-mastery and empowerment, lifting us out of a victim mindset, so we understand ourselves as strong, creative beings, more than capable of building the brilliant lives we desire.

This is a powerful way of living. Positive energy attracts energy that vibrates on the same level, which means that when we think positively and feel good, we attract more of the same into our lives.

Chapter Twenty-Eight

The Physiology of Happiness

"The 'normal' experience of the body and its aging is a conditioned response—a habit of thinking and behaviour. By changing your habits of thinking and behaviour; you can change the experience of your body and its aging."
— Deepak Chopra

There's real science behind these ideas.

Being positive and feeling good affects your nervous system. As we discussed, when you're in "fight, flight or freeze," your body is flooded with adrenaline. This is the sympathetic nervous response. When you're in the sympathetic response, your body shuts down or slows all systems that aren't immediately necessary for surviving trauma. So your immune system, your digestion, and your body's ability to repair itself are all "put on hold."

While these actions are slowed down, adrenaline and cortisol fill your body, increasing heart rate and blood pressure, and reducing your capacity for higher thought.

Imagine living in these conditions every day. That's what negativity and constant, low levels of stress inflict on us.

But when we feel positive, that's all reversed! The parasympathetic nervous system kicks into gear, reducing your heart rate and blood pressure, allowing your immune system to operate at full strength, increasing blood flow throughout your brain, and giving your body a chance to repair and restore itself. You're literally healthier when you feel good!

Positive thinking actually changes our biology. Research proves that our thoughts and emotions affect our stress levels and heart rate. The heart has a powerful magnetic field, radiating three to four feet out of the body. This field affects anyone who comes into its range.

Human beings are always communicating with each other, even when words aren't being spoken. The space between two people is not empty. It's full of energy—alive, vibrant, and influential.

When you're happy, your heart rate changes, and so does the magnetic field surrounding your heart. This positively affects anyone in that field. Their heart rate actually synchronizes with yours, meaning your heart and another's really do "beat as one." Positivity is contagious!

We should make a commitment to feeling good, because our bodies crave what we feed them. There's a biological reason for this. If you eat a piece of chocolate, your brain releases pleasurable hormones. These hormones are distributed through your body via your blood, and are taken in by your cells. Your cells use these hormones like energy, and when they burn through that energy, they crave more of the same. Your entire body literally craves more chocolate!

This is true for any food we eat, any substance we use, and any actions we repeatedly take. Everything we do releases chemicals from our brains, which feed our cells, and which our cells come to expect. Even if an action makes us feel bad or abused—like allowing a frustrated boss to yell at us—our cells come to expect the hormones released by that verbal abuse, and to crave more.

In addition to your cells, your brain grows accustomed to experiences and emotions, too. The brain is a very "elastic" organ, meaning it's capable of learning new things and changing its neural pathways in response to different stimuli. Every time you take an action, neural pathways in your brain are formed. Doing something for the first time always feels a little awkward and uncomfortable. And of course it is! Your brain has no neural pathways for the situation! It doesn't understand what you're asking it to do.

Do the same thing a second time, and your brain is a little more comfortable. At least it has a frame of reference to work from, now.

Do the same thing repeatedly, and the neural pathways in your brain become very strong indeed. It becomes easier and easier for you. That's why "practice makes perfect."

That's also why it can be so hard to break habits and addictions. That's one reason we continually repeat old patterns of behavior, even if we know they're not good for us and won't change our lives for the better. We live the patterns our brains and our bodies understand. Too bad for us if those patterns are negative, or not aligned with our brilliant purpose. No wonder the seven lies are so deeply engrained in us!

The good news is, we can teach our bodies and our brains to crave better food. Not only literal food, but experiences and emotions. So your cells crave what you continually give them? Give them something new and unexpected—something that releases happy hormones. You may find your body develops a taste for it more quickly than you expect. Take the same action repeatedly, and you'll find yourself with a new habit your body asks for every day.

Research indicates it takes about 90 days to develop a new habit. So stick with it, and soon it'll feel like second nature.

A good place to start is with imagination and visualization. These are powerful tools, because they allow you to mentally and emotionally live the life you desire. They allow you to feel the good without having the specifics in place … yet.

Intentionally visualize stepping over the threshold of your dream home, and you'll feel some pretty strong emotions.

These feed your body, and forge pathways in your brain, just like actual experiences.

The moment you choose a new version of you, your entire world will shift. You can start this process with powerful "I am" statements that speak to who you are and what you are becoming.

I AM a powerful creator of my own experience.

I AM feeling freer every day.

I AM deserving of my dreams.

Chapter Twenty-Nine

Pleasure Creates Profit

"I still have my feet on the ground; I just wear better shoes."
— Oprah Winfrey

Being happy and thinking positively can generate more profit for your business, too. In *Molecules of Emotion*, author Candace Pert proved that a single good thought produces cascades of "feel good" chemicals in our bodies. Of course, this changes your heart rate and the way you affect others. But when it comes to business, feeling good is a truly unstoppable force.

According to one study, CEOs can boost performance by 15%, and staff can increase customer satisfaction by 42%, simply by focusing on the positive and staying happy. The research puts numbers behind the common sense—it's much more pleasurable to interact with happy, smiling, engaging people than those who seem dour and uninspired.

So how happy do you have to be before you start to see results? Well, if everyone's feeling happy already, the rise in productivity will feel like the cherry on top (a very sweet cherry!). But in studies, a ratio of 3:1 positivity-to-negativity proves to be the tipping point that takes people and teams from average to flourishing. That means that feeling good and experiencing pleasure three times more than you feel down is one of the most important ingredients in success.

Most people aren't quite there yet. A ratio of 2:1 positive-to-negative emotions is more common. What can we do to raise our spirits (and our profits)?

"I am" statements and affirmations continue to be a powerful tool. Another one that can change your entire outlook, and the way you experience life, is meditation.

Meditation is difficult to define, because it has so many applications and benefits, but one of Deepak Chopra's most potent definitions of meditation is "a tool for the re-discovery of the body's own inner intelligence." Meditation is the practice of clearing our mind of clutter. It is the practice of connecting with silence, and listening to spirit and intuition. It can put us in deeper touch with our bodies, our higher selves, our guides, and more. It can aid healing in a number of ways, such as by activating the parasympathetic nervous system, and it can foster a deep sense of peace that helps us transcend the regular tumult and stress of everyday life.

Meditation has been proven to lower blood pressure, improve heart rate, release tension from overworked muscles, enhance brainwaves, and deepen healthy breathing. Brain scans done on people meditating show increased activity in the areas where metabolism and heart rate are housed, and studies done on Buddhist monks show that meditation boosts conscious perception, attention, learning, and memory.

Studies show that women experiencing PMS or menopause can reduce their symptoms by 58% due to meditation. There's even proof that meditation affects infertility. In one study, women struggling with infertility underwent a 10-week meditation program. 34% were able to become pregnant in six months, and mothers who meditated on images of milk flowing from breasts actually experienced an increase in their milk supply by more than 50%.

With meditation, we even have the power to communicate directly with the various systems and cells of our bodies.

You don't have to spend hours every day perched on a cushion with your feet balanced on your knees and your eyes closed.

All you need to do is take a little time daily to breathe deeply and empty your mind—let go of the constant stream of thoughts that fills your head all day, every day. Think of it like shutting down a computer and rebooting it.

Quieting that stream of thoughts can be difficult, especially if you're new to meditation, so go easy on yourself. Anytime a thought appears in your mind, acknowledge it and gently release it. Some people prefer to give their minds something to focus on, so it's easier to quiet all the other noise in their head. Focusing on the breath is a popular choice. If you go this route, just pay close attention to the length and depth of each breath, and feel the oxygen flowing to every nook and cranny of your body. You can also use a mantra or affirmation—a statement you repeat to yourself over and over.

Of course, you can use any mantra that appeals to you, but here are a few affirmations to get you started:

I have clarity, focus and vision for my life.

There is nothing that I hide from.

I take the time that I need to nourish me.

The Passing of the Warrior

"You haven't yet opened your heart fully, to life, to each moment. The peaceful warrior's way is not about invulnerability, but absolute vulnerability–to the world, to life, and to the Presence you felt. All along, I've shown you by example that a warrior's life is not about imagined perfection or victory; it is about love. Love is a warrior's sword; wherever it cuts, it gives life, not death."
— Dan Millman

The masculine Warrior energy has gotten the human race a long way since our hunter-gatherer days. We have a great deal to thank it for. Business, in particular, has been driven by warrior energy.

But the balance has long been out of proportion between masculine and feminine in the world. Now, feminine Goddess energy is rising to guide the world into a new era. It can feel like a struggle at times—and it's only natural that the Warrior won't step down without a fight.

However, the Warrior isn't so much stepping down, as he is coming into balance with the Goddess. He's coming to respect her, honor her wisdom, and look to her for leadership. This rising of feminine energy is going to change the way the world relates to itself. And it's women like us—who fight for our freedom and live our brilliance—who are making it happen.

About the Author

Dawn Todd is the CEO and founder of Wildly Successful Women and author of The Feminine Intention. With over twenty years in entrepreneurial ventures, Dawn has a proven track record for success as a life and business coach. She has also spent over 10,000 hours empowering people to choose their best life.

Dawn's stellar list of partners have included the Rockies Venture Club,
Angel Capital Summit,
eWomenNetwork,
Constant Contact,
American ExpressMicrosoft,

The Napoleon Hill Foundation and WomanScope News.

Wildly Successful Women creates over 100 face-to-face networking events annually. Dawn is a regular speaker for Constant Contact, and was the first women to chair Rockies Venture Club Angel Capital Summit.

Dawn and her husband have seven daughters. Visit her at www.dawntodd.com

Made in the USA
Monee, IL
10 May 2023